OCCASIONAL PAPER **137**

The Lao People's Democratic Republic

Systemic Transformation and Adjustment

D1405250

Edited by Ichiro Otani and Chi Do Pham

with contributions from
Jonathan G. Anderson, Michael Braulke,
James A. Daniel, Filippo Di Mauro,
Przemyslaw Gajdeczka, and Padma Gotur

INTERNATIONAL MONETARY FUND
Washington DC
May 1996

Cataloging-in-Publication Data

The Lao People's Democratic Republic systemic transformation and adjust-
ment / edited by Ichiro Otani and Chi Do Pham; with contributions from
Jonathan G. Anderson . . . [et al.]. —
Washington, D.C. : International Monetary Fund, 1995
    p.   cm. — (Occasional Paper ; 137)

   ISBN 1-55775-560-4

   1. Laos — Economic Policy. I. Otani, Ichiro. II. Pham. Chi Do.
III.Series: Occasional paper (International Monetary Fund) ; no.137.
HG443.L36   1996

Price: US$15.00
(US$12.00 to full-time faculty members and
students at universities and colleges)

Please send orders to:
International Monetary Fund, Publication Services
700 19th Street, N.W., Washington, D.C. 20431, U.S.A.
Tel.: (202) 623-7430   Telefax: (202) 623-7201
Internet: publications@imf.org

recycled paper

Contents

Preface

This Occasional Paper reviews the Lao People's Democratic Republic experience with systemic transformation and macroeconomic adjustment in recent years and highlights challenges that the country is likely to face in the coming years. This paper draws largely on background work carried out by the IMF staff missions for the 1994 Article IV consultation discussions with Lao officials and for policy dialogues with them in connection with the IMF financial assistance provided to the country under the enhanced structural adjustment facility over the 1993–96 period. This Occasional Paper, a product of collaborative efforts, has been edited by Ichiro Otani and Chi Do Pham. The principal contributors of sections are as follows: Ichiro Otani and Chi Do Pham (Section I); Michael Braulke (Section II); Michael Braulke and Chi Do Pham (Section III); Padma Gotur (Section IV); Jonathan G. Anderson (Section V); Filippo Di Mauro (Section VI); James A. Daniel (Section VII); and Ichiro Otani, Padma Gotur, and Chi Do Pham (Section VIII). Appendices I, II, III, IV, and V are contributed principally by James A. Daniel, Przemyslaw Gajdeczka, Michael Braulke, Filippo Di Mauro, and Chi Do Pham, respectively.

Many individuals have assisted in preparing this Occasional Paper. We wish to thank David Goldsbrough and Jeremy Carter for their insights and comments, Youkyong Kwon and Viola Chou for research assistance, and Mila Villar, Amparo Rosario, and Cathy Song for secretarial assistance. We also thank Thomas Walter for excellent editorial assistance and coordination of production.

The views expressed here, as well as any errors, are the sole responsibility of the authors and do not necessarily reflect the opinions of the Lao Government, the Executive Directors of the IMF, or any other members of the IMF staff.

1 Introduction and Summary

This paper assesses the experience of the Lao People's Democratic Republic (P.D.R.)[1] with systemic transformation during 1989–94, when the IMF provided financial support under the structural adjustment facility (SAF) and the enhanced structural adjustment facility (ESAF), and highlights challenges that the country is likely to face in the coming years in conducting macroeconomic management and making further progress in structural reforms. In this connection, the paper provides brief background information on the country's political history and economic developments during the period preceding the systemic transformation, with a view to contributing to a better understanding of the Lao experience with systemic transformation against its unique historical and political background.

Following a protracted civil war lasting two decades (1955–74), the Lao P.D.R. was declared in 1975, replacing the earlier monarchy, and a centrally planned economy was established. Although some private sector activity was maintained, the economic system was highly regulated. Farmgate prices and trade in agricultural products were administratively determined. Trade among provinces was restricted, and food coupons for public employees were usable only in state shops. In addition, the industrial sector—producing less than 15 percent of GDP—was largely composed of state-owned enterprises under the state planning system. These enterprises had to transfer annual targeted amounts to the budget, regardless of their financial performance, and often had to borrow heavily from the banking system to finance current operations.

The results were disappointing. Domestic price controls and tight restrictions on foreign trade led to the emergence of parallel markets for goods and foreign exchange. Meanwhile, a distorted incentive structure created supply shortages. Moreover, a lax monetary policy, which accommodated borrowing requirements of the state enterprises, fueled rapid inflation.

In 1979, in response to the disappointing economic performance, the Government started liberalizing trade and farmgate prices and depreciated the exchange rate. In 1985, the Government turned more decisively toward market-oriented polices under the system called the New Economic Mechanism (NEM). Public enterprises were given operating autonomy with regard to production levels, product mix, investment, employment, and wages. Agricultural procurement prices were freed, farmers began to receive payments in cash for their produce, and the state monopoly over the procurement and distribution of rice was terminated. Moreover, retail prices, except for certain public utilities and domestic air transportation, were liberalized. In addition, the private sector was authorized to participate in the production and distribution of most goods and services, while the scope of private and mixed enterprises in international trade was expanded. Finally, the exchange system was simplified, as multiple official exchange rates were unified at a level close to the parallel market rate.

During 1985–88, the Lao Government concentrated on further liberalizing prices and trade, both domestic and external, so that production, consumption, and investment decisions by economic agents could be increasingly based on market signals and private incentives. During 1989–91, the Government focused on establishing macroeconomic stability by tightening credit and increasing budgetary control. During 1992–94, while continuing a fairly tight monetary policy, the Government placed more emphasis on fiscal adjustment through both revenue-enhancing and expenditure-containing measures. At the same time, structural reforms were accentuated, notably in the areas of (i) banking, including the development of monetary instruments; (ii) privatization; (iii) trade liberalization; and (iv) improvement of the legal and regulatory framework to meet the needs of the emerging private sector. Table 1 summarizes the structural reform and policy measures implemented during the 1985-94 period.

Despite the progress achieved so far, several structural bottlenecks continue to hamper the full development of the country's economic potential.

---

[1] Formally known as Laos before December 2, 1975.

Table 1. Chronology of Structural Reforms and Economic Policy Measures, 1985–94

Action	Date
I. Production, Distribution, and Prices	
Autonomy granted to public enterprises to determine production levels and product mix, investment, employment, and wages.	1985–88
Government procurement prices freed.	Mid-87
Most retail prices freed.	10/88
Internal trade liberalized.	1986–87
Private sector authorized to participate in producing and distributing most goods and services.	1987–88
Private sector rights, including long-term land rental, autonomy of private firms, and the retention of after-tax profits, established.	3/88
First state-owned enterprise—a steel metal factory—privatized through leasing.	5/89
Decrees on arbitration, bankruptcy, and secured transactions enacted.	7–10/94
Privatization of 60 state-owned enterprises.	1989–94
II. Budgetary Policies	
Revenue	
First major tax reform enacted, including (i) replacement of state-owned enterprises' transfers to to the budget with profit and turnover taxes; (ii) establishment of profit tax on manufacturing in the 20–85 percent range; (iii) establishment of turnover tax on service enterprises in the 1–15 percent range; (iv) introduction of taxes on export profits in the 50–80 percent range; and (v) reduction of maximum import tax rate from 200 percent to 70 percent.	3/88
Log export tax introduced.	3/89
Second major tax reform, aimed at correcting design problems of the first, implemented. It included (i) replacement of export tax on gross income with specific export taxes applied to selected exports (timber, animals, and certain scrap metals) and an ad valorem tax at 80 percent on electricity exports; (ii) unification of multiple corporate income tax at 45 percent for nonbank enterprises and 60 percent for banks; (iii) introduction of turnover tax on services, wholesale trade, and imports, with five rates in the 3–20 percent range; (iv) extension of personal income tax to all salaried workers, including civil servants, with a progressive schedule in the 2–30 percent range; (v) introduction of specific ad valorem taxes on exploitation of natural resources; and (vi) introduction of land tax on nonagricultural land.	6/89
Permanent unit established at Ministry of Economy to monitor budgetary revenues.	6/90
Number of turnover tax rates in the 5–10 percent range reduced from five to two.	2/91
Excise taxes on petroleum products and luxury goods introduced.	2/91
Registration tax introduced.	9/91
Timber royalties restructured.	10/92
Land tax on agricultural and urban land replaced agriculture tax.	12/92
Minimum profit tax (approved in February 1991) implemented at 1.5 percent of turnover.	1/93
Export tax on agricultural products eliminated.	6/94
National registry of enterprises established for tax collection purposes.	6/94
Granting of "special conventions" in lieu of regular tariff payments terminated.	8/94
Number of import tariff bands reduced from 11 to 6, with rates in the 5–40 percent range, plus exceptional rates.	1/95
Fiscal Management	
Expenditure priorities reordered, including elimination of consumer subsidies and subsidies to civil servants and autonomous enterprises.	3/89
1989 budget ratified by the first elected Supreme People's Assembly.	6/89
Fiscal centralization adopted, and central and provincial budgets consolidated into a general government budget.	8/91
National Treasury established.	8/91

Table I (continued)

Action	Date
1992 budget submitted consistent with framework of centralization and treasury appropriation.	3/92
Revised treasury accounting system adopted.	6/94
Budget Law defining steps for budget preparation approved.	7/94

III. Financial Sector Policies

Action	Date
Two-tier banking system initiated with separation of central bank and commercial banking functions of the State Bank.	3/88
Two branches of State Bank transformed into independent commercial banks (Sethathirath Bank and Nakhoneluang Bank).	10/88
Preferential interest rates for public corporations and state cooperatives eliminated.	10/88
Interest rates on deposits increased from 5.4–15 percent to 7.2–18 percent.	10/88
Short-term lending rates increased from 4.2–8.4 percent to 10–15 percent.	10/88
Long-term lending rates increased from 3.0–4.2 percent to 6–10 percent.	10/88
New deposit and loan instruments introduced on which commercial banks can set interest rates subject to a ceiling of 12.5 percent a month on deposits and 15 percent a month on loans.	10/88
Improved monetary data reporting format introduced.	2/89
Actual deposit rate paid on new instruments increased from 3 percent a month to 5 1/2 percent; lending rate increased from 6 percent a month to 6–7 percent.	5/89
State Bank granted sole right to determine and manage the official exchange rate for foreign exchange on the basis of transactions in foreign exchange markets.	7/89
Market determination policy established for interest rates. Interest rates should be higher than inflation, loan rates should exceed deposit rates, and long-term deposit rates should exceed short-term rates.	7/89
Use and issuance of checks at State Bank and commercial banks inaugurated.	8/89
Interest payments permitted on foreign currency deposits at banks.	10/89
Joint Development Bank established (30 percent ownership by Lao Government and 70 percent ownership by Thai investors).	10/89
Banque pour le Commerce Extérieur Lao granted independence from State Bank.	11/89
Government bonds issued with State Bank as issuing agent.	1/90
Pak Tai Bank established, with offices in Champassak, Saravane, Xekong, and Attopeu.	4/90
Central Bank Law approved establishing Bank of the Lao P.D.R. as central bank.	6/90
National currency (kip) used for all domestic transactions; guidelines for foreign exchange transactions implemented.	9/90
Lao May Bank established.	9/90
First privately owned licensed foreign exchange dealer opened.	1/91
Lane Xang Bank established.	2/91
Aroun May Bank established.	9/91
Bonds issued by Bank of the Lao P.D.R.	11/91
Rules governing operations of commercial banks and credit cooperatives established.	1/92
Credit window opened to commercial banks for short-term credit at Bank of the Lao P.D.R.	1/92
Recapitalization of six state-owned commercial banks completed by replacing nonperforming loans worth KN 18 billion with a cash infusion (KN 4 billion) and treasury bills (KN 14 billion).	9/94

IV. External Sector Policies

Action	Date
New exchange rates introduced for private transactions; commercial exchange rate at which most official transactions took place devalued.	10/85
State monopoly on trade in most goods eliminated; permission to import granted to mixed and private companies.	1985–88

Table 1 *(concluded)*

Action	Date
Exchange rates further devalued; number of rates reduced from seven to four.	9/87
Official exchange rate adjusted in line with movements in parallel market rate.	9/87
Exchange rates unified at level close to parallel market rate.	1/88
Import tariff rates reduced.	3/88
New foreign investment law explicitly allowing profit and capital repatriation adopted.	7/88
New Foreign Investment Code promulgated.	7/88
Spread between official and private rates reduced to below 10 percent even during temporary pressure on rate in parallel market.	2/89
Implementation guidelines for Foreign Investment Code issued.	3/89
Restrictive practice arising from bilateral payments arrangement with two IMF member countries eliminated.	5/89
Export quota on high-quality logs introduced.	6/89
Difference between official and parallel market exchange rates reduced to 5 percent.	6/90
List of strategic goods exportable only by state trading companies reduced. Nonbank foreign exchange dealers authorized; restrictions on foreign exchange holdings removed; and foreign exchange surrender requirements eliminated.	9/90
Bilateral payment arrangements with former CMEA countries eliminated.	1990–91
Quantitative restrictions and specific licensing requirements for most goods eliminated.	2/91
New customs code with revised tariff rates adopted.	2/91
New foreign investment code adopted.	3/94
New customs law adopted; tariff structure further simplified.	1994–95
V. Civil Service Reform	
Civil service employment rationalized.	1988–89
Civil service reform process begun with goal of reducing overall cost and upgrading quality of civil service.	Late 89
Freeze placed on new hiring.	11/92
Major salary reform implemented revamping salary structure and reclassifying personnel in accordance with qualifications.	4/94

First, because of the low domestic resource mobilization, the country is still heavily dependent on external assistance. Second, the narrow production and export base—with export earnings depending mainly on electricity, garments, and timber and wood products—makes the economy vulnerable to external shocks and limits development prospects. Third, acute absorptive capacity problems delay the buildup of social and physical infrastructure. Fourth, the early fruits of economic development have remained concentrated in urban centers and have not reached the rural areas, where poverty is still pervasive. (See Box 1 for a discussion of poverty and social issues in the Lao P.D.R.)

The rest of the paper is organized as follows. Section II provides a brief historic description of political and economic developments through the late 1980s, emphasizing the essential geopolitical features of the country and the rich cultural heritage of its people, and highlighting experience with the reforms during 1979–88. The main finding of the section is that the process of liberalization started in 1979 and continued with the important reforms under the NEM, making the Lao P.D.R. one of the earliest systemic reformers among the former centrally planned economies.

Section III summarizes the main economic objectives and policies under the two subsequent medium-term adjustment programs supported by the SAF and the ESAF, respectively, during 1989–94. These policies represented a major overhaul of the economic system, affecting virtually all sectors of

Box 1. Poverty and Social Issues

As is to be expected in an economy with a per capita income of only about $350, a large rural sector, and weak infrastructure, poverty is widespread in the Lao P.D.R. According to the preliminary result of an extensive expenditure and consumption survey conducted in 1992 and 1993, roughly half the population lives in or near poverty, with a somewhat higher occurrence in the south than in the north, and with a much higher incidence in the rural sector than in urban centers.

Given the limited resources available for improving social infrastructure, government spending on education and health has been very low in the past. Total per capita expenditure on education and health in the 1994/95 budget reached just $15 and $6, respectively, which is among the lowest in the region. The long-standing underfunding of health and education is clearly mirrored in poor levels of key social indicators. While the Government's "education for all" policies—launched in the late 1980s with support from the Asian Development Bank, the World Bank, and bilateral donors—have made some headway in reducing adult illiteracy, in particular among younger females, the overall rate is still high by international standards, at an estimated 36 percent of the adult population. In the health area, some progress was also made as the infant mortality rate continued to decline over the past decade. However, both child and maternal mortality rates have remained stubbornly high, partly reflecting malnutrition and, particularly in remote areas, limited access to health services. To reach the standards of neighboring countries, much more needs to be done. A comprehensive strategy to address the situation remains to be formulated, awaiting the findings of the World Bank's social sector review. Meanwhile, the Government continues to reorient public spending toward the development of human resources. As is evident also from the latest rolling public investment program covering the period 1995–2000, its efforts focus on increasing central government allocations on social services and, with a view to improving delivery to rural areas, on physical infrastructure. Another government aim under this program is to improve recurrent financing of the social sector at the provincial level.

economic activity; they were successful in their aim of shifting the economy to reliance on market mechanisms.

Section IV reviews experience with controlling inflation during 1989–94. The sources of inflationary pressures in the early period and the policy response, in particular the successful implementation of monetary policy, are highlighted. The section also notes that, as inflation was reduced and monetary aggregates brought under control, new instruments of indirect monetary management were introduced, and steps to modernize the financial system were taken.

Section V shows that one of the main results of economic liberalization was to enhance the country's outward orientation. Trade reform, a liberal foreign exchange system, and a stable exchange rate have together contributed to the opening of new export markets.

Section VI discusses experience with fiscal adjustment during 1988–94, noting an early apparent success in fiscal consolidation in the early 1990s. However, the section points to some weaknesses in the consolidation process, particularly those related to patterns of revenue mobilization and the large wage bill.

Section VII notes that, as the economic liberalization progressed, the Government recognized in the late 1980s the urgent need to reduce public sector involvement in state-owned enterprises. The section also describes the Lao P.D.R.'s experience with privatization, including the nature of the public enterprises being privatized and the privatization methods adopted. In addition, the section argues that, despite some success, problems arose from the reliance on leasing as a dominant form of privatization and from the lack of a well-defined strategy.

Section VIII assesses the past reform efforts, underscoring the factors that have contributed to the promotion, as well as the hindrance, of the reform process. This section also identifies major areas of systemic reform that require significant efforts by the Government, thus highlighting the major challenges that the Government will face in the coming years.

This paper is also accompanied by five appendices, providing detailed discussions on (i) real exchange rate movements and external competitiveness; (ii) experience with foreign direct investment; (iii) the process of legal and constitutional reform; (iv) the structure of the tax system; and (v) the Government's policy agenda in the second half of the 1990s.

II Setting of Economic Reform

The Country at a Glance

The Lao P.D.R. is a landlocked, largely mountainous country in the center of the Indochina peninsula. Rugged terrain and elevations separate the country from Myanmar to the northwest and China to the north, and much of the Annamite chain stretching along its eastern flank acts as a natural barrier to Vietnam. The Mekong River, however, has served traditionally as a connecting link to Thailand to the west and Cambodia to the south.

The country is characterized by pronounced ethnic, cultural, and linguistic diversity. Reflecting primarily the altitudinal stratification of settlement, one classification differentiates the Lao people roughly as Lao Loum ("valley Lao"), Lao Tai and Lao Theung ("mountainside Lao"), and Lao Soung ("mountaintop Lao"). The Lao Loum, often referred to simply as "Lao," originated in southern China and settled along both sides of the Mekong River and its principal tributaries. Forming the largest single group, with a share in total population estimated at between one third and one half, the Lao Loum have traditionally played a significant role in culture and politics.

With an area of about 237,000 square kilometers and a population estimated at some 4.5 million (Table 2), the Lao P.D.R. is as large as the former Federal Republic of Germany or the United Kingdom, but it is sparsely populated—particularly in the mountainous north and east—in comparison with neighboring countries or the rest of Asia. Most of the people live in farming areas in the lowlands. However, spurred by the Vietnam War and an extended period of internal political struggle, urbanization has been proceeding rapidly. Whereas just 8 percent of the population was urbanized in the mid-1960s, today about 20 percent of the Lao people live in cities, notably the capital of Vientiane, which contains roughly half of the urban population.

About 60 percent of the country is estimated to be covered with dense tropical forests, and only about 10 percent of its area is considered arable. Actual cultivated area is just under 15,000 square kilometers, including some 6,000 square kilometers classi-fied as "shifting cultivation" land. The transportation system is generally weak, and major areas remain virtually inaccessible during the rainy season. Agricultural production is, therefore, still largely subsistence oriented. Furthermore, because only a fraction of the arable land is irrigated and most farmers lack access to improved inputs and essential technology, yields are low and depend heavily on the weather. Rice is by far the most important crop, accounting traditionally for over 80 percent of planted acreage. The country is, however, barely self-sufficient in food production and has repeatedly had to resort to imports.

The proportion of forests that are largely intact in the Lao P.D.R. is one of the highest in Asia. Forestry products were, therefore, traditionally among the few major foreign exchange earners. During the past 25 years, however, forest resources have declined rapidly. The rate of exploitation accelerated in the second half of the 1980s, when demand from neighboring Thailand for these resources rose steeply following that country's imposition of a logging ban. To reverse this trend, the Lao Government has recently reduced the number of logging permits drastically. (For a discussion of environmental issues in the Lao P.D.R., see Box 2.)

Combined with forestry, agriculture is estimated to employ 90 percent of the labor force and to account for 60 percent of GDP. Indirectly, agriculture accounts for even more of GDP, as much of the Lao P.D.R.'s small industrial sector processes agricultural products. Besides agricultural processing, the hydropower industry, which is another major foreign exchange earner, and the nascent garment industry, which thrives on foreign investment seeking to surmount textile quota hurdles, contribute significantly to the economy. The entire industrial sector accounts for little more than 15 percent of GDP.

In contrast to many other low-income countries with estimated GDP per capita of about $300, the Lao P.D.R. is well endowed with natural resources. It has untapped reserves of agricultural land, large forests, hydropower potential, and mineral resources that, when efficiently exploited, could contribute substantially to economic progress. However, the

Table 2: Economic and Social Indicators: Lao P.D.R. and Neighboring Countries

	Cambodia	China	Lao P.D.R.	Myanmar[1]	Thailand	Vietnam
Area (in thousands of sq. km.)	181	9,561	237	677	513	332
Agricultural land (in percent of total)	21	53	7	16	47	21
Population (in millions)	9	1,176	5	45	59	71
Density (persons per sq. km.)	51	123	19	66	115	214
Urbanization[2]	12	27	20	26	24	20
Agricultural employment (in percent of total)	...	56	86	65	57	72
GDP per capita (in U.S. dollars)	194	367	358	...[3]	2,102	166
Exports per capita	4	78	52	15	622	40
External debt per capita[4]	...	60	103	121	449	57
Share of state enterprises in nonagricultural employment (in percent)	...	39	6	5	13	19
Life expectancy at birth[5] (in years)	51	69	51	60	69	67
Infant mortality[6]	116	31	97	72	26	36
Child (under age 5) mortality[6]	169	38	158	100	31	44
Access to safe water[2]	...	78	29	33	72	50
Adult illiteracy[7]	65	27	42	19	7	12
Female illiteracy	78	38	67	28	10	16
Primary school enrollment ratio	...	125	101	102	114	103
			(Average 1990–93 growth, in percent)			
Population	2.5	1.2	2.9	2.2	1.5	2.3
Urban	4.8	2.2	6.3	3.4	4.4	3.2
Real GDP	6.8	11.4	5.7	3.6	7.8	7.4
Agriculture	3.9	0.9	-4.3	3.0	3.0	3.8
Industry	11.4	8.0	12.4	3.8	11.4	10.8
Consumer price index	123.3	8.1	9.8	28.5	4.4	39.8
Broad money	74.9	29.6	41.6	31.1	17.9	41.7
Exports (in U.S. dollars)	4.6	13.9	43.4	12.2	16.9	18.1
Real effective exchange rate[8]	...	-4.4	6.0	23.6	-0.4	3.9

Sources: Lao authorities; and World Bank and IMF staff estimates.
[1]Data refer to fiscal years starting April 1.
[2]In percent of relevant population.
[3]Per capita income was $1,232 at the official exchange rate and $66 at the parallel market rate.
[4]Excluding debt to the nonconvertible area.
[5]Based on 1992 data.
[6]Per 1,000 live births.
[7]Based on 1990 data; in percent of relevant population.
[8]Positive entry indicates appreciation.

country also faces very serious disadvantages. Its landlocked position, rugged terrain, low population density, and widely dispersed settlements generate high transportation and communications costs and render broad, equitable improvements in social and economic infrastructure expensive. Furthermore, the country continues to suffer from the adverse impact of the war, including the loss of lives and the exodus of a large number of skilled laborers. Therefore, the authorities face the difficult task of promoting economic development aimed at spreading benefits evenly throughout the country.

Brief Political History

The written history of the Lao P.D.R. begins in the fourteenth century with Fa Ngoun, called the Conqueror, who, with Khmer assistance, conquered the small states of the present-day Lao P.D.R. and much of northeastern Thailand. In 1353, he united these territories into the Lao kingdom of Lan Xang ("million elephants"), then one of the largest states in the region. Fa Ngoun established Buddhism as the state religion, but this had initially little effect on the animistic majority of the population. After years of

Box 2. Environmental Issues

Owing to the modest size of the industrial and mining sectors, environmental concerns in the Lao P.D.R. are chiefly related to the agricultural and forestry sectors, particularly in four areas: (i) forestry resource management; (ii) biodiversity conservation; (iii) land resource management; and (iv) water resource management.

Forestry resource management. The Government has been experiencing increasing difficulty in forest resource management as it has been unable to control effectively the depletion of forest resources. Although forest coverage in the Lao P.D.R. remains one of the highest in the world, forest depletion took place at unsustainable rates in the 1970s and 1980s, as wood extraction and encroachment by the farming population increased rapidly. In addition, returns from such depletion only partially accrued to the Government, owing to widespread illegal logging, clandestine exports, and inadequate pricing. Thus the Government, with World Bank assistance, now aims at striking a balance between sustainable wood production and environmental protection, particularly in areas in which watersheds and biodiversity are at risk.

Biodiversity conservation. Although the vast areas of intact forest in the Lao P.D.R. still allow one of the richest original habitats in the world, forest depletion had an increasingly damaging impact on the nation's rich biodiversity. Only recently did the Government approve legislation for wildlife protection and for the creation of a system of 17 protected areas, and the approach taken so far suggests that the legislation still relies primarily on command-and-control policies. The Government plans to place an increasing emphasis on providing proper incentives for the indigenous population to participate in conserving biodiversity. In order to secure the long-term support from the international community for conservation activities, the Government will consider steps to establish a conservation trust fund.

Land resource management. Even though the scarcity of land resources is not a pressing issue, use of land in the Lao P.D.R. is suboptimal. In the northern regions of the country (the uplands), population pressures on marginal land and the decrease of rotation periods are the root causes of land erosion and degradation of soil fertility. In the south, the lack of an integrated research and extension system constrains land yields to well below potential. Overall, irrigation facilities are not well developed in the lower uplands. The optimal regional and geographical specialization of agriculture—food production in the lowlands and tree plantations in the uplands—appears far away.

As in the case of forestry management, community-based resource management will be increasingly emphasized. At the same time, efforts will be made at the national level to provide policymakers with a better mapping of the overall land resources available, including the status of degradation and provisions for best land use. Concurrently, land legislation would allow a flexible allocation of land to farmers, based on land characteristics, labor availability, and possible uses, rather than maintain fixed upper limits.

Water resource management. The Lao P.D.R. is endowed with the highest per capita availability of renewable fresh water in Asia. However, with the development of hydropower schemes and increased urbanization, two serious problems may develop. First, the power projects may endanger the water catchment. Second, because of ineffective water management, coupled with insufficient resources devoted to water supply and sanitation, particularly in urban areas, water may become hazardous to public health. To deal with such potential problems, the Government is reviewing the overall environment assessment of hydroelectric projects and of comprehensive plans for water supply and sanitation improvements.

constant warfare that exhausted his people, Fa Ngoun was eventually driven into exile. His successor, a devout Buddhist, consolidated the administration, built schools and temples, and succeeded in making Lan Xang an important center of trade. Struggles with Siam and Burma began. Except for a brief period of anarchy and Burmese domination, however, Lan Xang's territory and power continued to grow until the end of the seventeenth century. Its rise culminated in the long reign of Souligna Vongsa, from 1637 to 1694, at times called the golden age of the Lao P.D.R.

After Souligna Vongsa's death, the kingdom disintegrated into three separate states: a kingdom based in Vientiane but under the suzerainty of Annam; an initially independent kingdom established at Luang Prabang; and a third kingdom, Champassak, which controlled the southern provinces along the Mekong but increasingly fell under the influence of Siam. After the occupation of Vientiane by Siam in 1778, both the kingdoms of Vientiane and Luang Prabang had to pay tribute, if only symbolic, to Siam. Later, the two kingdoms also had to pay tribute to the emperor of a rising Vietnam. The decline accelerated in the early 1800s as Vientiane engaged in a disastrous war with Siam, which eventually led to the destruction of the capital city, the forcible resettlement of its inhabitants, and the virtual depopulation of much of the central Mekong region. Additional Siamese campaigns also depopulated vast areas between the east banks of the Mekong and the Annamite chain.

After first recognizing Siamese suzerainty over the Lao region, France responded to a request by the court of Luang Prabang for protection toward the end of the nineteenth century by pressuring Siam to renounce all claims on territories east of the

Mekong. About 1900, France unified the administration of the main Lao principalities in Vientiane and allowed only the royal house at Luang Prabang to retain its title and prerogatives. Laos, as it was called, remained a French protectorate virtually through the end of World War II. At war's end, however, France recognized Sisavang Vong, who had been ruling Luang Prabang since 1904, as king of an autonomous Laos. In 1947, elections to form a constituent assembly were held, and the country's first Constitution was promulgated. Two years later, Laos became an independent associate state of the French Union and was eventually granted full sovereignty in October 1953.

From the onset, the newly independent country faced serious political and military difficulties. The Royal Government, headed by Prince Souvanna Phouma, encountered opposition from the Neo Lao Haksat (the Lao Patriotic Front), a dissident, communist-supported movement chaired by Prince Souphanouvong, a half-brother of Souvanna Phouma. The Pathet Lao, the military arm of the Patriotic Front, gradually seized control of the northeast provinces bordering North Vietnam, and, despite numerous attempts to reconcile the warring parties, Laos was de facto partitioned by the mid-1960s. As the Ho Chi Minh Trail ran through Pathet Lao territory, both sides were deeply drawn into the Vietnam War, and it was only in the context of the 1973 Paris peace agreement that a cease-fire in Laos was concluded. In April 1974, a new coalition Government was formed, and Prince Souvanna Phouma retained the post of Prime Minister while Prince Souphanouvong was appointed Chairman of the Joint National Political Council. However, in the ensuing months, the Patriotic Front steadily increased its power base by enlarging the Pathet Lao-controlled zone. Following the fall of Phnom Penh and Saigon in the spring of 1975, the Patriotic Front gained full control. When it won the elections in November 1975, King Savang Vatthana abdicated, and Prince Souvanna Phouma resigned.

Convening in December 1975, the National Congress of People's Representatives abolished the monarchy, changed the country's name from Laos to the Lao People's Democratic Republic, and elected a 45-member legislative body, the Supreme People's Council. Souphanouvong was appointed President of the Republic and of this council, and Kaysone Phomvihane, a leading figure of the Lao People's Revolutionary Party, became Prime Minister.

The Stage for Economic Reform

In the mid-1970s, the Lao economy shared many characteristics of centrally planned economies. However, certain special factors in the country's political and economic background both set the stage for economic reform and heightened its urgency.

Inheriting a war-torn and extremely underdeveloped economy in 1975, the leadership was faced with the formidable task of reconstruction and development. The crisis was heightened by the abrupt termination of U.S. aid and the disruption of cross-border trade resulting from the economic blockade of neighboring Thailand, the country's major trading partner and a key source of basic foods. At the same time, the Government experienced various setbacks in implementing measures designed to lay the foundation of the "socialist transformation" of the economy. For instance, the introduction of taxation and the collectivization of agriculture met with considerable peasant resistance, and adverse weather compounded the agricultural problems. Furthermore, as regulations increased, traders, entrepreneurs, professionals, and capital fled abroad. At the same time, a growing fiscal deficit and rapid monetary expansion, coupled with acute shortages, resulted in high inflation. The balance of payments position also deteriorated, reflecting the limited export expansion and the total dependence on bilateral agreements for import financing.

Thus, the first few years of the communist regime—the second half of the 1970s—offered little respite from falling living standards, stagnant or declining production levels, growing financial instability, and increasing internal resistance. Recognizing the inadequacy, if not total failure, of the economic measures patterned on the model of other centrally planned economies, the Government initiated a gradual move toward comprehensive economic restructuring, without abandoning its Marxist philosophy or adopting multiparty democracy, to tackle the nation's serious economic problems. Indeed, consistent with Marxist orthodoxy, the capitalist system was accorded a special transitional role and was viewed as a necessary intermediate stage on the path to socialism.

Early Reform Years (1979–88)

In December 1979, faced with a steadily worsening economy and under pressure from its creditors, the Government took its first tentative steps toward economic reform. The new policies stressed the need for increased efficiency and production, and assigned an important role to market forces and the private sector. Among the most important measures implemented were the removal of various restrictions on internal and external trade, the substantial devaluation of the national currency, the kip, and the dramatic adjustment of official prices, especially agricultural ones. The authorities hoped to draw

Chart 1. Excess of Free Market Prices over Official Prices, 1976–95

(In percent)

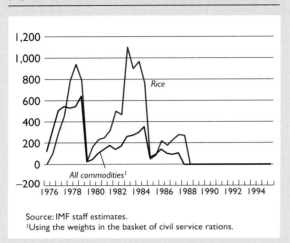

Source: IMF staff estimates.
[1]Using the weights in the basket of civil service rations.

unauthorized activities back into official channels and to revitalize the state sector. By restructuring, in particular, the grossly distorted agricultural price system, they also hoped to lay the basis for the country's First Five-Year Plan (1981–85), which aimed at reaching food self-sufficiency and promoting a balanced and diversified agricultural structure.

However, it was with the introduction of the New Economic Mechanism (NEM) in 1985 that the reform process gathered momentum. Public enterprise reform was marked by the granting of operating autonomy to enterprises, which allowed them to determine production levels and product mix, investment, employment, and wages. Thus, the system of economy-wide production targets set by the Government was abandoned. Domestic and foreign private investors were given a major role in the economy. Private sector activity was allowed in most sectors, including rice production, and restrictions on internal trade were abolished.

In addition, the Government introduced changes in financial policy. Taken in isolation, these changes were hardly revolutionary, but they marked the beginning of a series of far-reaching policy reforms in virtually all relevant economic areas during 1985–88, as the country's development strategy shifted toward more of a market orientation and a liberalization of the economy.

Price Liberalization

The dramatic adjustments in official retail and wholesale prices, starting with a ninefold increase in the price for basic rice rations in April 1985 and continuing with an average 360 percent increase in most other controlled prices throughout the remainder of the year, initially changed little in the underlying system. Repeating essentially the pattern of the adjustment at the end of 1979, the 1985 price adjustments were just sufficient to bring official prices temporarily in line with free market prices. But as the latter continued to rise—fueled in part by the necessary increase in public sector wages—the gap between the two prices soon began to widen again (Chart 1).

The two-tier price system of market prices and generally much lower official prices continued to exist in 1985–89. The official prices were, in principle, set to reflect production costs plus margins, but owing to political and social considerations or inadequate accounting practices—including the application of a grossly overvalued official exchange rate—they often involved substantial subsidies. The subsidy element of the official price system grew even larger when vouchers redeemable at state shops were increasingly used for public sector payments in lieu of cash. For instance, during the period from mid-1985 to mid-1989, as much as 90 percent of public sector salaries and wages were paid in the form of so-called salary coupons that could be redeemed at state shops. Also, roughly 60 percent of official procurement purchases were made by issuing vouchers redeemable at state or cooperative shops.

The fundamental reform of public sector pricing came through a decree issued in June 1987. This decree abolished the practice of "cost plus" pricing for state enterprises by stipulating that prices had to be market determined and that, notwithstanding regional differences, there should in principle be but one price in a given market. More specifically, the decree stated that prices, except those of a few utilities, public services, and several key industrial products, should be freely negotiated between the parties to a transaction without interference from the Administration. As the basic consumer goods sold through state shops were not among the listed exceptions, the decree also signaled an end to the many related subsidies. However, in order to cushion the impact on civil servants and because an appropriate solution to their compensation still had to be formulated, the sale of subsidized goods to these employees continued until it was phased out over the period March–October 1988.[2]

The price reform also greatly affected agricultural procurement. After years of increasing use of barter

---

[2]Sales against salary coupons ended effectively in March 1989, when state stores were ordered to exchange the remaining coupons for cash. Many of the state stores were consequently closed.

transactions and payment with vouchers, procurement agencies had again to monetize their transactions. More significantly, however, the transition from cost plus pricing to market-oriented pricing implied substantial increases in procurement prices for most crops.

Trade Reform

Throughout the decade to the mid-1980s, the Government had sought to increase its control over domestic and foreign trade; as a result, the public distribution system had become increasingly dominant and exceedingly complex. At the national level, the Lao Trade Corporation was in charge of official external and wholesale trade, as well as rice distribution.[3] At the local level, procurement and distribution operations were handled by provincial offices in accordance with quotas established by provincial planning committees and at prices that, since 1982, partly reflected local conditions but also had to stay within limits set by the central authorities. At the retail level, the distribution system relied on an extensive network of state stores and cooperative shops that continued to expand through 1986.

Notwithstanding substantial unrecorded trade outside official channels, the state sector also dominated foreign trade. The state had reserved a monopoly on virtually all major exports and also on most imports, with the exception of imports made by so-called *sociétés mixtes* (joint public and private companies) or a few state enterprises that were authorized to retain a portion of their foreign exchange earnings. In view of the small share of free foreign exchange earned through untied exports, the allocation of foreign exchange turned inevitably into a complicated exercise that had to comply with the provisions of numerous bilateral trade and foreign assistance arrangements, leaving little room for flexibility.

In advance of the sweeping price reforms decreed in July 1987, the Government also liberalized the domestic and external trade system. In early 1987, the intricate web of state trading companies was consolidated, and administrative units were barred from engaging in, and interfering with, trade transactions. Shortly thereafter, provincial trade restrictions, most notably those relating to the movement of rice, were eliminated, and transportation, previously a monopoly of state and provincial enterprises, was opened to the private sector. Restrictions on foreign trade were also relaxed as, subject to licensing by the Ministry of Commerce, joint and private com-

panies were permitted to trade and transport all but specifically listed "strategic" commodities.[4] Most of these restrictions disappeared during 1988 with the effective decontrol of prices and the liquidation of the Lao Food Corporation, which had monopolized the procurement of rice and shared its distribution with the Lao Trade Corporation.

Exchange Rate Reform

The exchange rate system for transactions in convertible currencies, like the implicit exchange rate system for transactions with the nonconvertible area, was complicated. With the introduction of two further rates in 1985 and early 1986, there existed seven different exchange rates. These included a symbolic official rate of KN 10 per U.S. dollar; a commercial rate of KN 95 per U.S. dollar, at which most transactions by state enterprises were made; and several rates close to the then-prevailing parallel market rate of roughly KN 400 per U.S. dollar, which applied to transactions by the *sociétés mixtes* or the prefecture of Vientiane.

Reform of the exchange rate system initially lagged behind other reforms. In September 1987, the number of exchange rates was reduced to four. While the overall spread between the highest and lowest rates was not narrowed, this first step brought the exchange rates applicable to most transactions very close to the parallel market rate. Reassured by the stability of the kip in the parallel market during the months following these initial steps—it even appreciated slightly—the authorities then moved quickly to unify, effective January 1, 1988, all rates at one very close to that prevailing in the parallel market.

Public Enterprise Reform

Prior to the adoption of the NEM in 1985, state enterprises were run along the standard model of a command economy, with virtually no room allotted for managerial flexibility or autonomy. Selling and input prices, salaries, investment, reinvestment, financing, product mix, and output targets were all determined by central or provincial authorities in accordance with the plan, the budget, or the stipulations of a supervisory ministry or provincial authorities. All operating surpluses, if any, and most of the depreciation allowances had to be transferred to the budget,[5] which, in turn, provided most of the

---

[3]Rice distribution was carried out jointly with the Lao Food Corporation, which was established in 1982.

[4]These commodities comprised a number of major exports that were initially reserved for state trading agencies so as to comply with bilateral trade contracts with the nonconvertible area.

[5]Because actual operating surpluses frequently diverged from the plan, these transfers were often effectively financed by the banking system.

financing for the necessary working capital and investment. As a result, little distinction was made between state and public enterprise assets, and virtually no incentive existed to improve financial performance, let alone earn a reasonable return on investment.

The first attempts to accord Lao state enterprise managers at least some degree of autonomy were made as early as 1983 at four of the most important centrally supervised enterprises.[6] Two municipal enterprises and another two enterprises under provincial supervision were added to the experiment in 1985. Initially, greater autonomy at these enterprises meant merely the permission to retain 40 percent of profits and, in the case of the Lao Wood Industry Corporation, also most of its depreciation allowances. But gradually greater autonomy was accorded to other public enterprises, which, in turn, were expected to become financially self-sufficient. By the end of 1987, roughly 75 percent of all centrally owned enterprises were thus granted a considerable degree of operational freedom, as long as they conformed with the two main targets established for each enterprise under the plan: output and payments to the budget. As funding through the budget for such enterprises had been discontinued by that time, the annual plans gained additional significance as the principal basis for justifying requests for credit from the banking system.

Fiscal Reform

Even though a tax system had been in place before the public sector reforms began, the principal source of domestic budgetary revenue used to be negotiated transfers from state enterprises. As increased financial autonomy was extended to a greater number of state enterprises, the revenue system had to be adjusted; accordingly, the authorities announced in a decree of June 1986 that the largely inoperative tax system would be overhauled and simplified.

The tax reform was implemented with the 1988 budget. Contrary to the initial intention, however, the new tax system turned out to be complicated and highly differentiated. Depending on the type of activity, the flat tax on commercial and industrial profits derived from domestic sales ranged from 20 percent to 85 percent, while profits derived from export activities were to be taxed at rates ranging from 0 percent to 80 percent, with some activities subject to a lower rate and others subject to a higher rate than the corresponding domestic activity. Like the profit tax, the turnover tax and the new import tariff system, which came into effect in March 1988, were

highly differentiated, with rates ranging from 1 percent to 15 percent and from 1 percent to 70 percent, respectively. Moreover, wages and salaries of Lao citizens working for Lao employers remained untaxed, while the agricultural income and profits tax was maintained (although its rates were slashed again, to a yield-dependent rate of 4–5 percent in the case of paddy[7] and to 6 percent for all other agricultural production).

Parallel with the attempts to adjust the revenue system, efforts were made in 1988 to reorder expenditure priorities. As subsidies to civil servants and other consumer subsidies were gradually phased out, civil service wages were raised, although not in step with the resulting price increases. At the same time, and helped by an early retirement scheme and the introduction of separation payments, a substantial retrenchment of central government staff began.

Banking and Financial Sector Reform

Reform of the financial system lagged far behind those in other areas. In October 1988, the separation of central and commercial banking activities of the State Bank started. The Nakhoneluang Bank became autonomous, and two large branches of the State Bank in Vientiane were split off one year later as independent commercial banks. The process continued with the creation of several other commercial banks.

Interest rate policy, which was still within the authority of the Council of Ministers (the cabinet of the Lao Government), also changed little. In October 1988, the traditionally low deposit rates were raised by 20–50 percent, and the lending rates were roughly doubled. At this time, the authorities also abandoned the distinction between private and public sector with regard to credits and deposits and terminated the extension of preferential terms to the public sector. Most interest rates remained negative in real terms, and deposit rates, in particular, proved too low to enable the newly founded commercial banks to compete effectively with rates offered in the curb market.

Summary of Structural Reforms and Macroeconomic Developments

The implementation of major reforms during 1979–88 represented substantial progress in moving toward an open and market-oriented economy. The reforms helped to reactivate private sector activity and improve the quantity and range of goods available in the domestic market. The services sector was

---

[6]These were the tobacco and beer factories, the electricity company, and the Lao Wood Industry Corporation.

[7]Although the agriculture tax was generally progressive with respect to yield, its rate structure was highly regressive at both ends of the yield spectrum.

the quickest to respond to the improved incentives: private and public transport operators took advantage of the removal of internal trade restrictions, while enterprises involving handicrafts and consumer services (repair shops, tailors, and restaurants) quickly emerged as a result of the liberalization of private activities.

This favorable impact on macroeconomic performance was, however, largely offset by several adverse developments. In the late 1980s, the dismantling of the system of transferring surpluses of public enterprises to the budget caused a drop in revenues and an increase in government dissaving, while the decentralization of decision making was followed by local governments' action to provide large wage increases financed by bank credit. Accentuated by the effects of a prolonged drought in 1988, these developments triggered a surge in inflation, a large current account deficit, and the depletion of foreign reserves. The authorities were unable to manage the new system effectively because of the absence of the necessary policy tools, including indirect means of monetary management control and an adequate institutional framework.

Clearly, much remained to be accomplished in the transformation process, as subsistence farming and barter continued to characterize the agricultural sector and the public sector still dominated the monetized economy. Moreover, despite sizable public investments during the late 1970s and early 1980s, economic and social infrastructure remained inadequate, and the existing capital stock was poorly maintained and often obsolete. Domestic saving remained low, as the private sector made only limited use of the banking system. On the external side, exports, which covered only one third of imports, were narrowly based, while foreign reserves were low.

III Recent Macroeconomic Performance and Structural Reforms

Against the background summarized in the previous subsection, the Government adopted a major medium-term adjustment program in 1989, followed by another in 1993. This section summarizes the main objectives and reform strategy pursued during the period 1989–94, as well as the performance of the Lao Government under the programs. Sections IV–VII examine in greater detail economic developments in each of the major policy and reform areas.

First Medium-Term Structural Adjustment Program (1989–92)

Objectives and Reform Strategy

In mid-1989, the Government resumed a medium-term adjustment program with support under the IMF's structural adjustment facility (SAF) and a World Bank structural adjustment credit, with the objective of establishing domestic and external financial stability while implementing the structural reforms. Specifically, the program aimed to (i) achieve an average annual rate of real GDP growth of 5–6 percent; (ii) reduce the rate of inflation by 1992 to that prevailing in major trading partner countries (about 5–6 percent); and (iii) make progress toward balance of payments viability.

The 1989–92 program was framed to tackle a wide range of issues. To promote production, the program envisaged an improvement in producer incentives, accompanied by actions to rehabilitate productive enterprises and improve the socioeconomic infrastructure. In this connection, private sector investment was promoted by privatizing state-owned enterprises and introducing a legal framework for foreign direct investment, while public sector investment was undertaken by the Government with assistance from the donor community. The increased investment was to be financed by additional foreign resources and expanded public and private sector savings. To enhance domestic resource mobilization, the tax system was to be reformed, the finances of public enterprises improved, and financial sector re-

form initiated. To restrain demand pressures, the program emphasized the need to adopt cautious demand-management policies that entailed the elimination of bank borrowing by the Government and the curtailment of credit to state enterprises. Finally, to strengthen the external position, the exchange rate was to be managed flexibly, the trade and payments system further liberalized, and the contracting of new nonconcessional external debt strictly limited.

Policies and Performance

Macroeconomic Policies

With a view to achieving the medium-term macroeconomic objectives, the Government initiated a number of steps in macroeconomic policy areas. In the fiscal area, a fundamental reform of the tax system was begun to reflect the increased autonomy of state-owned enterprises, equalize tax treatment between the public and private sectors, and introduce tax incentives for foreign investment. On the expenditure side, priorities were substantially reordered. In particular, consumer subsidies and subsidies to civil servants and to enterprises were eliminated. The role of monetary policy was confined to limiting the state-owned enterprises' demand for credit and credit expansion by the banking system. In the external area, the official exchange rate was set generally at a rate close to the parallel market rate, while the trading system was rationalized further.

Macroeconomic Performance

A strong recovery of rice and electricity production in 1989 from earlier drought-stricken levels was followed by continued buoyant growth, apart from a small drop in rice production in 1991. At the same time, the relatively small construction and manufacturing sectors witnessed strong growth as domestic and foreign investors responded to the new opportunities opened up by the reforms. The pickup in output growth, along with the tightening of financial policies, brought about a dramatic reduction in the inflation rate (end-of-period basis) from about

82 percent in 1989 to about 10 percent in 1991. The rate fell further to about 6 percent in 1992, largely reflecting the continued pursuit of prudent demand-management policies and a bumper harvest. This improvement occurred despite a large increase in electricity tariffs and rents during the year (Table 3 and Chart 2).

The external position strengthened considerably during 1989–92. Early on, export receipts were boosted by a rebound in electricity sales to Thailand and growing timber earnings, and, in 1992, by a strong growth in garment exports. With buoyant exports and a slowdown in import growth (owing to tighter domestic financial policies and the underimplementation of capital expenditure), as well as higher private transfer flows attracted by a renewed confidence in the Government's policies, the current account deficit contracted by 2 percentage points of GDP. At the same time, stepped-up aid inflows from multilateral and bilateral donors more than offset the sudden loss in 1991 of financial assistance from the former Soviet Union. Although the overall balance shifted into deficit in 1991 as a result of temporary delays in program loan disbursements, a surplus position was restored in 1992. Gross foreign reserves of the banking system almost quintupled from $17 million at the end of 1988 to about $80 million at the end of 1992, equivalent to four-and-a-half months of total imports, although official reserves remained at only two months of imports. The increasing proportion of highly concessional debt and the improvement in exports facilitated a decline in the debt-service ratio from 20 percent in 1988 to under 15 percent in 1992.

Structural and Institutional Reforms

Agricultural decollectivization and price liberalization were the most important structural reforms introduced because they permitted a long-overdue adjustment of relative prices in favor of agricultural products. Also, contractual and leasing systems affecting land tenure were introduced.

Financial sector reform entailed the establishment of a two-tier banking system in June 1990, with the promulgation of the Central Bank Law establishing the Bank of the Lao P.D.R. as successor to the old State Bank. The central bank's instruments of monetary management were expanded gradually over 1989–92. During this period, the extension of banking services and improved management of commercial banks bolstered confidence in the banking system and were instrumental in mobilizing domestic savings, increasing financial intermediation, and attracting foreign capital.

State enterprise reform, together with privatization, required hard budget constraints on enterprises

(which had previously monopolized bank credit) and severed the link between enterprises and the budget. In 1989, the Government announced its plan to privatize all but about a dozen strategic state enterprises.[8] During 1989–90, several enterprises were privatized on an ad hoc basis without sufficient regard to maximizing financial returns. Drawing on the lessons of that experience, a wider program of privatization, involving leasing arrangements, auctions, joint ventures, and improved bidding procedures, was adopted in 1991. Divestiture was rapid at the provincial level, with some larger provinces divesting (in many cases through sales to workers) over two thirds of the small enterprises under their jurisdiction; even though the privatization procedures adopted were less than optimal, this still represented significant progress. However, only limited progress was made in privatizing large and medium-sized state enterprises, where the procedural and administrative problems and the shortage of trained staff seriously hampered negotiations with foreign investors.

In the external area, the authorities built upon actions that had already yielded considerable benefits by further liberalizing the foreign trade system and the foreign investment regime. All exports and imports other than those on specified lists were freed from quantitative restrictions. As of the end of 1992, only timber exports remained subject to quantitative restrictions (for environmental reasons), and only imports of rice and certain types of motor vehicles still required quantitative licensing.

The Government also made some progress in institution building, although it was constrained by the lack of skilled staff and administrative delays. An important action was the promulgation of a new Constitution in August 1991, the first since 1975, which laid the foundation for the adoption of various business laws and important changes in the regulatory framework. The drafts of a number of such laws were prepared but still await enactment. In addition, the Government launched a major administrative reform in early 1992 aimed at streamlining decision making and reducing staffing, but progress has been slow.

Second Medium-Term Structural Adjustment Program (1993–95)

Objectives and Reform Strategy

The objectives and basic strategy embodied in the first medium-term adjustment program for the pe-

---

[8]Subsequently (in 1995), the Government decided to keep 32 state enterprises in its hands.

Chart 2. Overall Macroeconomic Performance

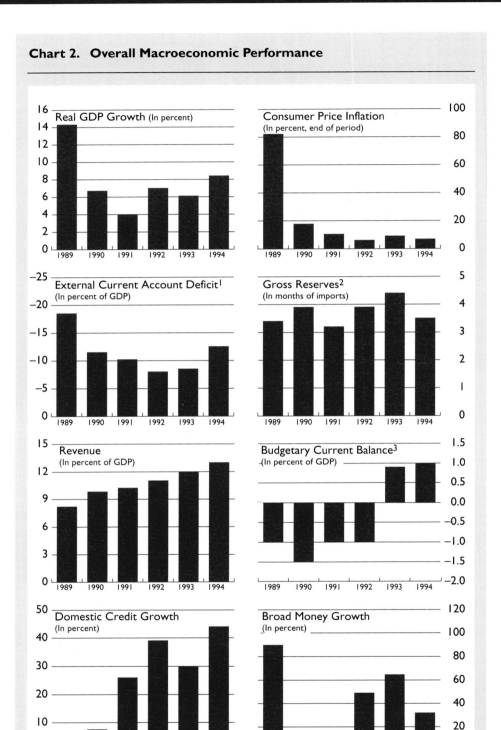

Sources: Lao authorities; and IMF staff estimates.
[1]Excluding official transfers.
[2]Gross reserves of the banking system.
[3]Excluding grants.

Table 3. Economic and Financial Indicators

	1985	1986	1987	1988	1989	1990	1991	1992	1993	1994
	(Annual percent change, unless otherwise specified)									
National income and prices										
Real GDP	6.9	9.2	−2.9	−0.7	14.3	6.7	4.0	7.0	6.1	8.4
Agriculture	7.4	9.4	−1.9	−4.2	10.8	8.7	−1.7	8.3	2.7	7.6
Industry	12.0	6.6	−16.0	−2.4	35.0	16.2	19.9	7.5	10.3	8.7
Real GDP per capita	4.0	6.2	−5.6	−3.5	11.0	3.7	1.0	4.0	3.1	5.3
Nominal GDP (in billions of kip)	76	124	210	235	427	613	722	848	986	1,159
Consumer price index (annual average)	106.0	37.1	6.0	14.4	59.5	35.7	13.4	9.8	6.3	6.7
Consumer price index (end of period)	136.8	15.0	9.8	13.0	82.1	17.7	10.4	6.0	9.0	6.8
External sector										
Exports, f.o.b.	22.4	2.6	12.9	−6.9	9.5	24.3	22.7	37.3	75.2	23.3
Imports, c.i.f.	19.3	−3.9	16.4	−24.9	29.7	−4.3	6.6	23.5	54.6	30.6
Nominal effective exchange rate	−2.8	−57.8	−2.1	−69.6	−37.3	−17.7	1.5	−3.5	−0.9	2.6
Real effective exchange rate	92.7	−42.2	1.8	−72.8	18.4	9.7	10.0	2.0	1.2	3.9
Kip per U.S. dollar (end of period)										
Official exchange rate	95	95	368	453	714	696	712	717	716	719
Parallel market rate	339	423	388	412	628	735	721	737	732	729
Government budget[1]										
Revenue and grants	91.0	64.3	5.8	93.1	27.4	60.1	27.8	17.4	26.5	30.6
Total expenditure	134.2	35.1	11.2	154.3	41.8	34.8	5.3	14.8	11.1	38.5
Current	129.1	56.6	8.3	75.0	42.4	74.9	17.3	23.1	9.5	20.5
Capital	139.2	15.2	14.9	248.7	41.4	10.7	−6.1	5.0	13.2	62.9
Money and credit[2]										
Net domestic assets	15.7	82.6	36.2	29.8	4.5	7.6	26.2	38.9	33.0	44.2
Broad money	35.6	70.0	79.0	37.1	89.7	7.5	15.8	49.0	64.6	31.9
Velocity (GDP/broad money at year end)	33.1	32.1	13.2	10.8	10.4	13.8	14.1	11.1	7.8	8.1
	(In percent of GDP)									
Government budget[1]										
Revenue and grants	16.2	16.2	10.2	17.5	12.3	13.7	14.8	14.8	16.1	17.9
Total expenditure	26.0	21.3	14.1	32.0	24.9	23.4	20.9	20.4	19.5	23.0
Budgetary current balance	1.1	3.0	1.9	0.2	−1.0	−1.5	−1.0	−1.0	0.9	0.8
Overall balance (cash basis)	−12.4	−6.5	−4.5	−19.8	−16.6	−14.4	−11.3	−11.7	−7.8	−11.0
External sector[3]										
Current account balance[4]	−5.6	−6.9	−9.8	−13.7	−15.8	−9.0	−4.3	−3.5	−2.2	−4.7
External debt outstanding[5]	9.6	13.1	14.9	34.4	32.5	35.7	32.9	34.8	36.2	36.8
Debt service [5]	0.8	0.8	1.0	1.7	1.6	1.1	1.2	0.8	0.7	0.7
	(In percent of exports)[6]									
External debt service[5]										
Including IMF	18.0	16.7	16.8	13.1	13.8	9.1	9.5	5.5	2.9	2.2
Excluding IMF	4.9	7.3	11.1	8.6	11.3	7.6	8.8	4.7	2.7	2.1
	(In millions of U.S. dollars)									
External current account balance[4]	−93.8	−90.6	−117.7	−79.2	−115.6	−77.8	−44.1	−41.0	−29.5	−72.5
Overall balance of payments	20.7	8.6	−11.3	−1.8	−4.3	−18.1	32.1	4.7	13.9	−10.1
Gross international reserves[7]										
(End of period)	25.9	32.6	21.2	29.4	59.8	64.8	57.2	85.8	150.9	158.2
(Equivalent months of imports)[6]	1.9	2.1	1.2	2.2	3.4	3.9	3.2	3.9	4.4	3.5

Sources: Lao authorities; and IMF staff estimates.

[1]Data from 1992 onward are adjusted to calendar-year basis from original fiscal-year (October–September) basis.

[2]1987 data are partly adjusted for a major change in the valuation of foreign-exchange-denominated assets and liabilities.

[3]Domestic currency values converted at official exchange rate (for commercial transactions). Data before and after 1988 are not entirely comparable, owing to massive realignment in the context of the exchange rate unification.

[4]Including official transfers.

[5]Excluding debt to the nonconvertible area.

[6]Exports of goods and nonfactor services.

[7]Including foreign exchange holdings of the banking system.

Box 3.   Trade Taxation

Prior to 1988, the system of trade taxation consisted of (i) an ad valorem import duty levied on the c.i.f. value of imports, ranging from 5 percent to 200 percent, with numerous exemptions; (ii) a turnover tax levied on imports of state enterprises and trading companies, ranging from 5 percent to 25 percent; and (iii) an export duty levied on the f.o.b. value of exports, ranging from 10 percent to 40 percent (the lower rates applied to private sector transactions), with a number of exemptions. The large number and wide dispersion of tariff rates, together with the then-existing system of multiple exchange rates, nonmarket price determination of trade with the CMEA, and proliferation of exemptions, implied a highly distorted system of incentives for external transactions. Initial steps to rationalize the system of trade taxation were undertaken in 1988–89. Direct export taxes were replaced in 1988 by a system of taxes on profits accruing from exported goods, at rates ranging from 2 percent to 80 percent. At the same time, maximum import duty rates were lowered from 200 percent to 70 percent. The unification of the official exchange rates unified prices in trade with the convertible area, although nonmarket prices continued to apply in trade with the nonconvertible area.

In 1989, a new customs code was adopted, together with a revised tariff structure, with 12 rates ranging from 2 percent to 80 percent. The customs code simplified and strengthened the legal framework for external transactions. However, fixed valuation prices were maintained for many goods, trade with the nonconvertible area remained subject to differential taxation, and the tariff regime was characterized by a myriad of discretionary exemptions that could be granted by various ministries and levels of government.

During 1993–94, the trade taxation system underwent further rationalization. Early in 1993, the Government replaced the taxation of export profits with a simplified system of royalties (applying primarily to timber and electricity). In 1994, the Government adopted a new Customs Law, which strengthened the commitment to a market-based system based on international norms. Significantly, the law formalized invoice-based valuation and adopted a strict definition of allowable exemptions, thereby eliminating the scope for discretionary policy.

In early 1995, the Government adopted a new tariff structure on the basis of the Harmonized Commodity Description and Coding System that had been introduced in 1993. The new tariff structure reduced the number of tariff bands from 12 to 6 and lowered the maximum rate from 80 percent to 40 percent (exceptional tariff rates above 40 percent were limited to three goods categories). The current tariff structure implies a low level of protection in comparison with other countries in the region. On a simple average basis, the average import duty in the Lao P.D.R. is 14 percent, while corresponding levels are 44 percent in Thailand, 12 percent in Vietnam, 20 percent in Cambodia, and 43 percent in China.

---

riod 1989–92 remained valid for the successor program, which was supported by arrangements under the IMF's enhanced structural adjustment facility (ESAF) covering the years 1993–95. Accordingly, the program aimed at maintaining high rates of growth and further improving financial stability, but the authorities also recognized the need to address several institutional weaknesses encountered during the first program period. To this end, reorienting public sector operations and completing the establishment of an effective, centralized system of fiscal management were made key priorities. Strong emphasis was also placed on advancing to more comprehensive and genuine forms of privatization, strengthening the commercial basis of the banking system, and building an adequate legal and regulatory framework.

Policies and Performance

Macroeconomic Policies

Not surprisingly, given that the thrust of macroeconomic policies during the ESAF arrangement period remained broadly unchanged from that during the SAF arrangement period, the Government continued to pursue macroeconomic policies characterized by a cautious, demand-management approach. Against this background, the Government aimed at further mobilizing domestic savings during 1993–94, mainly by achieving a net saving from the government sector (compared with a net dissaving over the SAF arrangement period). Accordingly, the Government took further revenue measures and contained current spending. At the same time, the authorities maintained a relatively tight monetary policy by keeping real interest rates substantially positive. These cautious financial policies supported the stability of the nominal exchange rate.

Macroeconomic Performance

Macroeconomic performance during 1993–94 was, on the whole, again remarkable. Despite a weather-induced shortfall in agricultural production in 1993, real growth averaged about 7 percent during 1993–94. Broad money growth surged temporarily to about 65 percent during 1993 before falling to

32 percent during 1994. Owing to a considerable decline in velocity, which reflected rising real rates of interest and increasing confidence in the banking system following the opening of several foreign banks, inflation settled at about 6½ percent in both 1993 and 1994. Fiscal performance remained mixed during the period, as bottlenecks continued to weaken administrative capacity, but the external sector performed better than targeted in many areas as exports and foreign trade in general continued to grow strongly, foreign private capital inflows surged, and foreign assistance reached record levels.

Structural and Institutional Reforms

Considerable progress was again achieved in implementing structural reforms during 1993–94. The state enterprise sector, which in the Lao P.D.R. had never reached the significance that it had in many other former centrally planned economies, was rapidly reduced in size. As most of the enterprises were privatized through ad hoc leasing arrangements, the outstanding issue now remains to implement procedures for complete divestiture. In tackling the sensitive problem of further streamlining the bloated civil service, the authorities had to overcome a number of problems, including a disappointingly low rate of voluntary separation, poorly targeted incentives, and uncontrolled hiring at provincial levels. After a reclassification exercise in 1994 that downgraded a number of staff, especially in the higher echelons, the authorities began to identify redundant and unqualified staff for retrenchment. In the area of fiscal management, progress in strengthening administration remained limited. Revenues also fell short of expectations because newly introduced taxes, such as the land and registration taxes, were not immediately implemented and because ad hoc tax breaks were increasingly granted.

In contrast, substantial progress was made in reforming the financial sector. The opening of private sector banks during 1993–94 contributed to increased competition while the state-owned commercial banks were recapitalized in 1994. Additionally, with the commencement of regular treasury bill auctions and the opening in 1994 of a discount window, the central bank made further headway toward installing the instruments of indirect monetary management. Finally, the significant progress made in achieving external sector reform culminated in mid-1994 in the elimination of the last remaining restrictions on international current account transactions. To streamline customs administration, the Harmonized Commodity Description and Coding System was introduced in 1993, and, after the adoption of the Customs Law in late 1994, the Government approved for implementation in early 1995 a comprehensive tariff reform package that halved both the number of tariff bands and maximum rates while ending the practice of granting exemptions on an ad hoc basis. (Box 3 summarizes the reforms in trade taxation made from 1988 to 1995.)

IV Monetary Policy and Financial Sector Reforms

Nominal anchors, in the form of either nominal exchange rates or predetermined rates of money growth, have proved to be useful in the process of disinflation in many developing countries or transition economies. However, the authorities in the Lao P.D.R. did not adopt these anchors during the period under review. Instead, the authorities adopted a strategy of targeting the growth in net domestic assets of the banking system, taking into consideration the balance of payments objective and the expected demand for money. This strategy was adopted even though the relationship between monetary aggregates and economic activity was unstable and the degree of currency substitution extensive. At the same time, in the initial period of the disinflation process, the authorities floated the exchange rate with a view to finding a rate that reflected market forces more accurately than the fixed or managed float system, and to unifying the official exchange rates once financial imbalances were reduced. In parallel with these policy initiatives, various forms of financial sector reform were undertaken.

The approach taken by the Lao authorities proved to be effective in reducing inflation while avoiding the significant decline in output that is often experienced in transition economies. What follows describes the experience with monetary policy and financial sector reforms since 1989.

Monetary Policy

Inflation Control

The pursuit of generally prudent monetary and credit policies has been a key factor since 1989 in restoring and later sustaining macroeconomic stability. In particular, during the early years of the SAF-supported program (1990–92), these policies played a key role in substantially reducing inflationary pressures. The policy stance was gradually tightened, with interest rates sharply increasing to positive real levels in the second half of 1989, and became progressively more stringent during 1990–91. Meanwhile, in the absence of fully effective indirect pol-

icy instruments, the authorities continued to rely mainly on traditional, direct instruments, including limits on currency issue and instructions to state-owned banks to reduce credit to state enterprises. These policies, together with the Government's low level of bank borrowing, were largely successful in halting the rapid growth in credit and reducing broad money growth from almost 90 percent during 1989 to an annual average of about 12 percent during 1990–91 (Table 4). The monetary tightening, together with efforts to strengthen fiscal discipline, facilitated a dramatic decline in the inflation rate from a peak of nearly 90 percent in August 1989 to under 18 percent, on a 12-month basis, by the end of 1990 and further to about 10 percent by the end of 1991 (Chart 3).

The authorities continued to pursue generally cautious monetary and credit policies during 1992–94, notwithstanding some acceleration in the growth of broad money in 1993 related to structural changes in the banking system (discussed below). These developments contributed to a substantial reduction in the velocity of money, which helped avoid any significant adverse effects of the rapid monetary growth on financial stability. Owing to these policies, as well as to continued efforts at fiscal tightening, the inflation rate declined to single-digit levels in 1992 and settled at about 6½ percent in 1993–94.

Progressive Strengthening of Monetary Control (1988–94)

In the years leading up to the adoption of the SAF-supported program in mid-1989, various factors contributed to the authorities' weak control over monetary policy. First, before 1989, the principal aim of monetary policy was to help fulfill the development plan. Thus, although policy was guided by a credit and currency plan, this plan was implemented flexibly, as additional credit requests by state enterprises to meet production targets and implement new projects were liberally approved. Second, even if the authorities intended to achieve a given monetary growth target, they lacked the effective tools to do so. In these circumstances, the central bank experi-

Table 4. Monetary Survey
(End-of-period data, unless otherwise specified)

	1988	1989	1990	1991	1992	1993	1994
	(In billions of kip)						
Net foreign assets	1.5	20.1	21.6	22.7	36.6	72.9	58.7
Net domestic assets	20.2	21.1	22.8	28.7	39.8	52.9	107.3
Domestic credit	26.5	26.7	31.1	44.1	56.1	74.7	128.9
Net credit to Government[1]	2.8	−14.3	−14.6	−0.9	0.6	−9.5	12.6
Credit to nongovernment sector	23.7	41.0	45.6	45.0	55.5	84.2	116.2
Public enterprises[2]	22.9	36.6	39.7	24.1	17.8	18.3	17.4
Private sector[2]	0.9	4.4	5.9	20.9	37.7	65.9	98.8
Other items (net)	−6.3	−5.6	−8.3	−15.5	−16.3	−21.8	−21.6
Broad money	21.7	41.1	44.3	51.3	76.5	125.8	166.0
Narrow money	12.1	25.1	25.1	28.2	35.1	52.2	61.3
Currency outside banks	3.5	16.8	...	19.2	22.8	33.2	38.6
Demand deposits	8.6	8.3	...	9.0	12.3	19.0	22.7
Quasi-money	9.6	16.0	19.3	23.1	41.3	73.6	104.6
Time and savings deposits	0.1	0.3	0.9	4.2	9.7	30.4	45.6
Foreign currency deposits	9.5	15.7	18.4	18.9	31.7	43.2	59.0
	(Percent change)						
Domestic credit	47.5	−3.3	16.3	42.1	27.1	33.2	72.5
Net credit to nongovernment sector	53.6	73.0	11.2	−1.3	23.3	51.7	
Of which: Net credit to private sector[2]	690.9	5.1	34.0	254.1	80.4	74.9	38.0
Broad money	37.1	89.3	7.8	15.7	49.0	64.6	31.9
Memorandum items							
Velocity of money (period average)[3]	12.2	13.6	14.3	15.1	13.3	9.8	7.9
Reserve money (in billions of kip)	...	20.4	22.1	26.3	36.9	60.7	74.2
Money multiplier[4]	...	2.0	2.0	2.0	2.1	2.1	2.2

Source: Lao authorities.

[1]Includes recording in commercial bank's balance sheets in 1994 of KN 5.3 billion worth of bonds out of KN 14 billion that were issued for recapitalization of state-owned commercial banks. Concurrently, bad loans amounting to KN 5.3 billion were removed from their portfolios.

[2]Reflects the reclassification of credit in the monetary survey from public enterprises to the private sector following privatization.

[3]Broad money divided by nominal GDP.

[4]Broad money divided by reserve money.

mented with direct instruments of control, such as credit-deposit ratios. Third, interest rates played only a small role in mobilizing and allocating resources and remained unchanged throughout 1979–85, despite sharp increases in inflation. Finally, the structure of the banking system was rudimentary. Prior to 1988, the banking system consisted of a single financial institution—the State Bank—and its provincial and district branches, which conducted both central and commercial banking activities. Administrative deficiencies also impeded the implementation of monetary policy, while statistical weaknesses complicated the analysis of related developments. These deficiencies in the institutional and policy framework contributed to the generally rapid expansion in monetary and credit aggregates in the second half of the 1980s.

Monetary Developments (1988–91)

Following a sharp wage adjustment in the public sector in late 1988 and the resultant heavy budget deficit financing in 1989, broad money rose by nearly 90 percent during 1989. Facing this situation, the authorities initiated several actions to tighten monetary control and reform the financial system. To slow monetary growth, they eliminated preferential access to credit by public enterprises and established an overall credit ceiling. Moral suasion was also used extensively to contain the growth of credit

Chart 3. Inflation and Monetary Developments

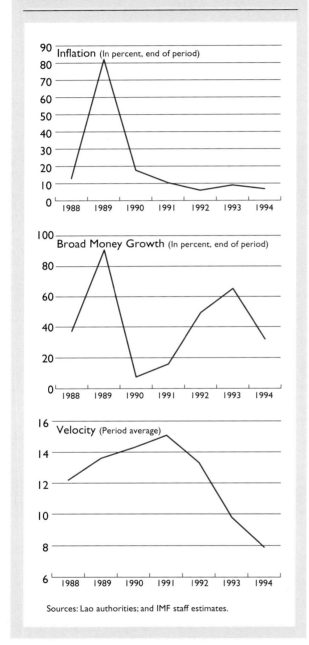

Sources: Lao authorities; and IMF staff estimates.

portant, the rate on the central bank's advances to the commercial banks was increased from 6 percent to 28 percent; the rate on one-year time deposits was increased from 14 percent to 36 percent; and a daily rate of 1 percent was imposed on overdrafts at the commercial banks (see Table 5 and the discussion below). Also, in November 1989, the central bank issued guidelines to banks and branches of the State Bank to observe a credit-deposit ratio of 70 percent. In the area of financial sector reform, the process of separating the central and commercial banking functions of the State Bank was initiated. Efforts were also intensified to improve the classification, coverage, and timeliness of monetary data.

Together, the above measures served to improve monetary control. The concurrent privatization of state enterprises also contributed to a drop in credit demand by this sector. These tightening efforts were sustained and brought favorable results in 1990–91. The growth rate of credit to the state-owned enterprise sector was cut dramatically, reducing sharply the growth of broad money to some 8 percent in 1990 and 16 percent in 1991.

Three points should be highlighted with regard to monetary policy in 1990–91. First, tight monetary policies did not impose an undue constraint on emerging private sector activity, largely because the credit squeeze was concentrated on the public sector. Second, the authorities did not revert to the use of quantitative credit ceilings but sought to enforce the targeted credit-deposit ratio through moral suasion alone. Third, while the authorities regarded guidelines for minimum interest rates and informal limits on credit to public enterprises as policy tools to be used during the transitional period, they recognized that indirect monetary instruments would better serve the needs of a market-oriented economy. Thus, as discussed further below, they initiated the development of such instruments, including bank reserve requirements in 1990–91.

Monetary Developments (1992–94)

Monetary developments in 1992–94 were affected by three main features: the impact of ongoing financial sector reforms, in particular the emergence of foreign banks; substantial declines in the velocity of money; and the development of, and greater recourse to, indirect tools of monetary management.

Monetary growth gathered momentum over this period, largely reflecting buoyant private sector activity and the related surge in credit demand. After accelerating to nearly 50 percent during 1992, monetary growth rose further to about 65 percent during 1993. This sharp increase was attributable to a combination of factors. First, rising real deposit rates on

to enterprises. Interest rates were raised substantially in July 1989 on bank deposits and loans—to real positive levels by the end of the year—and punitive rates were imposed on overdrafts. The authority to determine interest rates was transferred from the Council of Ministers to the central bank. Most im-

Table 5. Interest Rates
(In percent a year)

	1989 August[1]	1991 July[2]	1991 November[3]	1993 July[4]	1994 September
Deposit rates					
Demand	1.2	0.0–1.2	1.2		
Savings	24.0	16.0–20.0	12.0	12.0 (minimum)	12.0 (minimum)
Time					
3 months	30.0	18.0–24.0	15.0		
6 months	33.6	20.0–26.0	16.0		
1 year	36.0	24.0–30.0	18.0		
Lending rates[5]				24.0 (maximum)	24.0 (maximum)
Agriculture and forestry	28.0, 27.0, 27.0	15.0, 9.0, 7.0	14.0, 12.0, 10.0		
Industry and handicrafts	28.0, 27.0, 27.0	22.0, 12.0, 10.0	23.0, 18.0, 18.0		
Construction and transportation	29.0, 28.0, 28.0	25.0, 15.0, 12.0	25.0, 19.0, 18.0		
Commerce and services	29.0, 28.0, 28.0	30.0, 12.0, 10.0	26.0, 20.0, 18.0		
Agricultural Promotion Bank				10.0, 8.0, 7.0–15.0	10.0, 8.0, 7.0–15.0[2]
Overdraft	28.0	24.0	24.0	28.0	28.0
Bank of the Lao P.D.R. advances (credit window)					
Preferential projects[7]	2.0–12.0	2.0–12.0	2.0–12.0	26.0	26.0[6]
Rate paid on required reserves of banks held at the central bank	1.2	1.5	1.5	1.2	—[8]
Settlement account	1.2	1.5	1.5	1.2	1.2[8]
Treasury bills (6 months)					15.1[9]

Source: Lao authorities.
[1] Officially fixed rates.
[2] Guidelines for minimum and maximum interest rates.
[3] Guidelines for minimum interest rates.
[4] Revised guideline of July 5, 1993.
[5] The three rates refer to short-term, medium-term, and long-term loans, respectively.
[6] The credit window was replaced by a discount window in May 1994.
[7] On-lending of concessional borrowing by the Government.
[8] Effective December 1993.
[9] Weighted average of successful bids in the three auctions held in September 1994.

kip-denominated savings deposits sparked a sharp growth in time and savings deposits. Second, six foreign banks commenced operations in Vientiane, thereby boosting confidence in the banking system and encouraging the conversion into bank deposits of foreign currencies (Thai baht and U.S. dollars) that had been previously in circulation but not recorded as broad money. Finally, the rapid monetary growth also reflected to a lesser extent a one-time balance-sheet effect of the new banks' opening positions on their assets and deposit liabilities. In 1994, broad money expansion slowed markedly in line with the waning impact of some of these special factors, especially the entry of foreign banks.

The faster rates of monetary growth posted in 1992–94 should be viewed in conjunction with the sharp decline in velocity witnessed during this period. The steady decline in velocity from 15 in 1991 to 8 in 1994 helped to check the re-emergence of inflationary pressures.

During 1993–94, monetary control was exercised increasingly through indirect instruments. As discussed further below, the central bank made frequent discretionary adjustments in the cost of credit provided to commercial banks through its credit window, and, in mid-1994, it replaced the window with a discount facility to tighten the scope of such lending. In late 1994, to reduce the potential for further rapid credit creation arising from excess liquidity in the banking system, the central bank doubled the reserve requirement ratio and sought to discourage recourse to its overdraft facility by tightening the terms of such borrowing.

Monetary Instruments

The central bank has taken a number of steps to develop indirect instruments of monetary management. First, in October 1990, a minimum reserve requirement of 5 percent of specified liabilities was introduced. In November 1994, as noted above, this requirement was doubled to 10 percent in order to absorb excess liquidity in the banking system. Second, in January 1992, a formal credit window was opened at the central bank. Under this facility, commercial banks could borrow to meet their short-term liquidity needs. However, to strengthen monetary control and tighten the provision of central bank credit, the credit window was replaced by a discount facility at the Central Bank in May 1994. Third, in March 1994, treasury bill auctions were commenced on a regular basis. These last two measures, together with the further progress made in allowing market forces to determine interest rates, are expected to lay the foundation for liquidity management through open market operations and to contribute to the development of an interbank money market.

Interest Rate Policy

Since the second half of 1989, commercial banks have been given progressively greater autonomy in setting their own interest rates on deposits and loans within bands established by the central bank. The main objective of these guidelines has been to ensure that rates remain positive in real terms. Subsequently, the development of market-based instruments of monetary management, the easing of inflationary pressures, and the strengthening of the banking system have all combined to allow a gradual reduction in nominal interest rates and the removal of most interest rate guidelines. Interest rates have been decontrolled at a gradual pace in order to (i) allow banks to adapt to the more competitive environment and develop the skills and expertise needed to operate in the new market-oriented financial system; (ii) give banks the opportunity to increase their profitability and improve their financial positions; and (iii) allow the central bank time to improve its capacity for banking supervision and regulation.

In 1991, all interest rate ceilings were removed, but the minimum rate guidelines were retained for a period to ensure the maintenance of real positive interest rates (Table 5). In July 1993, in light of their continuing success in reducing inflation—which had fallen to single-digit levels in 1992–93—the authorities eliminated most of the minimum rate guidelines on deposit and lending rates. However, guidelines for minimum and maximum lending rates to the agricultural sector and a minimum rate on savings deposits were retained, while a maximum rate for loans was introduced.

Reform of the Banking System

Beginning in 1988, the Government implemented a series of measures to reform the banking system, with a view to making it more market oriented and improving the mobilization and allocation of resources. Several of these reforms were part of the SAF- and ESAF-supported adjustment programs.

Early Development of the Banking System

Prior to 1988, the financial sector had many of the characteristics of financial sectors in centrally planned economies. A single financial institution—the State Bank—conducted both central and commercial banking activities. The State Bank's principal operations were to accept deposits from state-owned enterprises and provide credit to them under the Central Government's economic plan; to act as the Government's treasury; and to manage the supply of currency.

Beginning in 1988, the financial sector underwent a major restructuring in the context of the NEM, as central bank activities were separated from the commercial banking activities of the State Bank. This separation began with the transformation of branches of the old State Bank into two autonomous commercial banks (Nakhoneluang Bank and Sethathirath Bank). In October 1989, the Joint Development Bank was established, constituting the first private sector participation in the banking industry, with 70 percent equity capital provided by Thai investors and 30 percent by the Lao central bank. In November 1989, the central bank's largest branch, the Banque pour le Commerce Extérieur Lao (BCEL), was granted autonomy, followed by the constitution of three more independent state-owned banks in 1990 (Pak Tai Bank, Lao May Bank, and Lane Xang Bank) from previous branches of the central bank.

The proper central banking activities of the State Bank were formally separated with the enactment of the Central Bank Law in June 1990, which established the Bank of the Lao P.D.R. as a central bank, established its role and functions, granted it the necessary powers, and assigned it primary responsibility to exercise control over monetary and financial developments. In September 1991, the two-tier banking system was further strengthened. First, the Aroun May Bank, the last remaining of the original four branches of the old State Bank, was turned into a commercial bank. Second, a centralized system of international reserve management was put in place by transferring assets from the BCEL—which had held most of the official international reserves—to the Bank of the Lao P.D.R.

The Bank of the Lao P.D.R. is now responsible for issuing currency; acting as the Government's banker and fiscal agent; acting as an agent for auctioning treasury bills; managing official international reserves; licensing and regulating financial institutions; and exercising prudential supervision of the financial sector.[9] It has the autonomy to conduct monetary and credit policy; act as a lender of last resort by extending short-term credit to commercial banks; set guidelines for interest rates; and formulate exchange rate policy.

In the past few years, the Lao banking system experienced further growth and a concomitant increase in competition with the entry of foreign banks. The first branch of a foreign bank (Siam Commercial Bank) commenced operations in December 1992,

followed by four new branches of foreign banks (Thai Military Bank, Thai Farmers Bank, Krungthai Bank, and Bangkok Bank) in 1993, and one (Ayoudya Bank) in 1994. A joint venture (Vientiane Commercial Bank) was also established in 1993, with 25 percent of the capital provided by Lao private investors and 75 percent provided by foreign investors. Finally, a new, entirely state-owned bank (Agricultural Promotion Bank) opened in July 1993, undertaking the role of servicing the agricultural sector. As of the end of 1994, there were eight state-owned commercial banks, two joint-venture banks, and six branches of Thai banks in the Lao P.D.R.

Emerging Role of the Commercial Banking System

The banking system has become more important in recent years because of a number of factors. First, the extension of banking services, together with the maintenance of substantially positive real interest rates, served to attract savings. Second, the entry of foreign banks and the actions to improve the management capabilities of commercial banks helped enhance confidence in the banking system. Confidence was further strengthened by the establishment in 1995 of nonbank foreign exchange bureaus and the resulting ability of residents to maintain bank accounts in foreign currencies.[10]

The financial sector traditionally was characterized by the absence of nonbank financial institutions—with the exception of the General Insurance Company, a subsidiary of a French company—and the lack of an established securities market. The latter deficiency was corrected in March 1994, when the primary market for treasury bills was instituted with the commencement of regular auctions of those instruments. Until recently, a large informal credit market, comprising mainly credit cooperatives, served to channel household savings to borrowers who did not qualify for loans from the formal banking system. The rapid growth of the commercial banking network has led to a shift of funds from credit cooperatives to banks; consequently, many cooperatives encountered serious financial difficulties and recently ceased to operate.

The range of banking services offered has expanded considerably in recent years. Since 1988, banks have begun to offer a range of deposit and credit instruments on a competitive basis and to provide basic services to their customers. Nonetheless, while the increased monetization in the Lao economy has fostered a rapidly expanding market for

---

[9]The Bank of the Lao P.D.R. is no longer involved in direct lending to the private sector, except to on-lend funds from multilateral organizations to the commercial banks.

[10]Effective mid-1995, the Bank of the Lao P.D.R. required that all foreign exchange bureaus be representatives of the commercial banks.

banking services, the banking system remains small in relation to the size of the economy.[11]

A prominent feature of the commercial banking system is its large degree of concentration. The three largest banks (the BCEL, the Nakhoneluang Bank, and the Sethathirath Bank) control about half of the system's assets and deposit liabilities. By and large, the BCEL maintains a dominant position, accounting for about 31 percent of the total assets and about 38 percent of the total deposit liabilities of the commercial banking system. The system is also characterized by a marked geographical concentration of banking services. State-owned banks operate on a regional basis, but, despite the gradual expansion of branches in rural areas, banking activities are concentrated in the Vientiane area. Each foreign bank is allowed to establish only one branch in the country and is restricted to operating in the Vientiane area.

Bank Recapitalization and Restructuring

The state-owned commercial banks have been burdened since their creation by a large number of bad loans to public enterprises and cooperatives that they inherited from the old State Bank. Nonperforming loans dominated their loan portfolios and seriously undermined their financial soundness. Thus, as a precursor to bank recapitalization, a survey of these banks' asset portfolios was initiated in 1990 to estimate the amount of bad loans and assess the amount of capital needed to bring the banks' capital base in line with the capital adequacy requirement of 8 percent of risk-adjusted assets specified by the Basle Committee on Banking Regulation and Supervisory Practices. This survey, completed in 1994, determined that approximately KN 18 billion (1.6 per-

cent of GDP in 1994) would be needed to recapitalize the state-owned banks. With financial and technical support from the Asian Development Bank, the financial viability of state-owned banks was strengthened with the cash injection of KN 4 billion in March 1994 and the issuance of KN 14 billion in government bonds in late 1994, and the subsequent removal of bad loans from the banks' assets. Relieved of the burden of bad debts and having established an adequate capital base, banks can now make the transition to competitive commercial operations and improve their bank management skills.

The problem of bad loans, on the one hand, and the granting of autonomy to commercial banks, on the other, have highlighted the importance of developing a prudential system. Recently, the Bank of the Lao P.D.R. initiated a number of measures to improve its capacity to exercise prudential regulation and supervision over financial institutions, with technical assistance provided by multilateral organizations and bilateral donors.

Future Monetary and Banking Sector Reforms

Notwithstanding the good progress made in financial sector reform, a number of challenges remain. First, the authorities will endeavor to ensure that the problem of bad loans does not recur by implementing a variety of measures, including a strengthening of bank management. Second, the monetary authorities need to develop expertise in indirect monetary management and in promptly adapting monetary policy to changing circumstances. Third, the complete liberalization of interest rates is on their agenda. Other tasks will include steps to develop an interbank market and a secondary market for securities and to introduce one comprehensive accounting system for the central bank and another for the commercial banks.

---

[11]This is illustrated by the very low ratio of the stock of broad money to nominal GDP, which, as of the end of 1994, was estimated at 1:8.

V Exchange Rate Policy and Trade Liberalization

Prior to 1985, when the Lao P.D.R. embarked on the new system of economic management, the exchange and trade regime was characterized by strong centralization. Trade operations were dominated by the state sector, where a small number of trading organizations and public firms held a monopoly on the bulk of exports and imports. The composition of trade was mainly determined by the Ministry of Commerce on the basis of national priorities, and foreign exchange was allocated according to planned needs through the central government budget or the BCEL. Exchange rates for official transactions were administratively determined and, in general, bore little relation to the scarcity value of foreign exchange. Market-oriented transactions were limited to the small private sector, which engaged in limited import and export operations and bought and sold foreign exchange on the parallel market, where rates were much more depreciated.

In addition, more than half of the volume of trade was accounted for by the nonconvertible area (primarily members of the Council for Mutual Economic Assistance (CMEA), and, in particular, the former Soviet Union). This trade was carried out on a bilateral clearing basis and was thus outside the system of exchange rates altogether.

On the Eve of Reform

During the early reform years 1986–87, trade arrangements were liberalized somewhat; the Lao authorities allowed the formation of joint-venture trade enterprises, the *sociétés mixtes*, which were permitted some autonomy in export and import operations. These enterprises were allowed to retain their foreign exchange earnings and were given access to official exchange markets at a rate closer to that prevailing in the parallel market. State exporting enterprises were also allowed greater retention of foreign exchange and broader access to import markets. As before, however, most trade remained firmly centralized; in particular, exports of a number of important "strategic" goods, undertaken primarily in fulfillment of trade contracts with the nonconvert-

ible currency area, continued to be reserved for state trading companies.

Initial reform efforts were accompanied by a proliferation of exchange rates; by 1987, external transactions were conducted at seven different rates, ranging from KN 35 per U.S. dollar and KN 95 per U.S. dollar for most official transactions to more than KN 450 per dollar for informal transactions through the parallel exchange market. This system was highly distortionary, deterred exports for a number of goods, and gave rise to shortages of goods and their administrative rationing.

Given the tentative nature of the early reform measures, trade performance remained subdued during 1986–87. The total value of exports increased at an annual rate of 6 percent—roughly the same rate of growth as in the pre-reform years 1982–85—owing primarily to increased exports of wood and wood products. Imports were even more sluggish, growing at an annual rate of 3½ percent during the same period.

Exchange Reforms and Exchange Rate Policy After 1987

Exchange Market Reforms

In order to stimulate exports, increase the share of foreign exchange transactions occurring at market rates, and channel a larger proportion of transactions through the emerging banking system, the Lao authorities began a dramatic reform of the exchange regime in late 1987.

The system of multiple exchange rates was eliminated, and a new, unified official rate was established at the beginning of 1988. The initial rates (KN 350 per U.S. dollar for buying and KN 380 per U.S. dollar for selling) were set close to the rates prevailing in the parallel market, representing a devaluation of nearly 400 percent for transactions of state enterprises (which were responsible for more than two thirds of the total trade volume) and lesser devaluations for private remittances and certain commercial transactions.

In tandem with the liberalization of trade (see below), the authorities also removed barriers to exchange market access in 1988. Virtually all current account transactions were freed,[12] and exporting firms were allowed to retain their foreign exchange earnings. With the adoption of a new foreign investment law in mid-1988, restrictions on foreign investment inflows, outward profit remittances, and the repatriation of foreign investment capital were also lifted.[13]

Further exchange market reforms were undertaken in late 1990, when the Government authorized the establishment of nonbank foreign exchange dealers and lifted restrictions on residents holding bank accounts denominated in foreign currency.

Exchange Rate Policy

Following the unification of the official exchange rate of the kip in 1988, the central bank has maintained a "managed float," adjusting the official rate broadly in line with the parallel market rate. Under this policy, the official rate was changed numerous times in 1988 and 1989, resulting in a cumulative depreciation of the nominal effective rate of nearly 50 percent. The difference between the official and the parallel rate for the U.S. dollar generally remained below 10 percent in domestic currency terms during this period (except during August–October 1989, when the differential widened to as much as 19 percent).

The exchange rate stabilized in late 1989 despite the continued high level of inflation; a slowdown in underlying monetary expansion, as well as substantial inflows of foreign exchange owing to the increased disbursement of external assistance, contributed to the achievement of this stability. From January 1990 through mid-1991, the authorities were able to revalue the official rate of the kip against the U.S. dollar, and the parallel rate also appreciated in nominal terms. From mid-1991 to the end of 1994, tight financial policies kept inflation down, and the Bank of the Lao P.D.R. maintained the official exchange rate at about KN 718 per U.S. dollar while accumulating foreign reserves. At the same time, liberal access to foreign exchange, together with a continued rise in the number of authorized banks and foreign exchange bureaus, minimized the difference between the parallel and the official exchange rates; the average spread was

2.7 percent in 1992 and less than 2 percent during 1993 and 1994.

Trade Liberalization and Performance After 1987

Trade Reforms

The partial trade reforms of 1986–87 were followed by a more fundamental liberalization of external transactions during 1989–90. In late 1989, the authorities widened the access of state and joint-venture firms to broad import licenses, which allowed the import of all but a small list of goods.[14] Then, in 1990, permission to engage in nonstrategic import and export activity was granted to all firms, whether state or private. Eligibility criteria for trade operations were limited to a registration procedure, whereby a potential exporter or importer obtained a permit from the Ministry of Commerce.

At the same time, specific licensing and quantitative restrictions were lifted on all but a small number of products. Such licenses are required for imports of petroleum, cement, steel, automobiles, motorcycles, rice, and a few locally manufactured items, as well as for exports of timber, wood products, rattan, coffee, and livestock. In practice, quantitative restrictions apply primarily to timber exports and motor vehicle imports.[15] In addition, the public sector monopoly on exports has been reduced to only two "strategic goods," logs and minerals, which only specially authorized public enterprises and provincial trading companies are allowed to export. All other goods can be freely exported (with proper licenses) by the private sector.

Trade Performance

Continued domestic liberalization and growth, together with developments in trading partner countries, have led to enormous changes in the size and structure of external trade. Major developments have been the collapse in trade with the former Soviet Union and other former CMEA countries (which had previously accounted for one third to one half of total trade), and the tremendous growth in trade with the convertible area, led both by rising exports of primary products and by a surge in trade in domestic manufactures and imported consumer goods.

During 1988–90, in addition to the trade liberalization discussed above, there was a substantial shift in the direction of trade from the nonconvertible to

---

[12]The major exception was a limit on travel allowances; this exchange restriction was removed in early 1994.

[13]Outward capital transfers by residents remain restricted; in practice, however, these restrictions have been only weakly enforced.

---

[14]Previously, licenses had been provided only to state trading companies and certain exporters.

[15]Quantitative restrictions on motor vehicle imports were removed in 1995.

the convertible currency area (Tables 6 and 7). The decision of the CMEA countries to discontinue providing their traditionally high levels of concessional financing led to a 50 percent decline in imports from the nonconvertible area from their peak in 1987. As a result, the trade deficit with the nonconvertible area declined from over $100 million in 1987 to $50 million in 1990.

This decline was offset by rapid growth in imports from the convertible area, which increased by 60 percent between 1987 and 1990 (Table 7). Much of this increase came from imports of petroleum, machinery, and raw materials, which were needed to make up for the decreased supply from the CMEA. In addition, imports of other categories (for example, consumers' goods) became more important during this period, reflecting the continued liberalization and the role of private importers in consumer goods trade. The trade deficit with the convertible area grew steadily from 1987 through 1990, financed to a large extent by the increased provision of aid and concessional lending.

The collapse of the CMEA in 1991 and the reorientation of the Eastern European economies toward market-based trade resulted not only in the termination of their bilateral trading agreements with the Lao P.D.R. but also in the complete disappearance of these markets for Lao exports and of financing for CMEA imports. As a consequence, total trade vis-à-vis the former nonconvertible area plummeted from over $90 million in 1990 to $4 million in 1992–94 (Tables 6 and 7); the latter figure comprises small amounts of coffee and metals that continue to be exported primarily to the former Soviet Union as payment for debt service. Thus, the withdrawal of CMEA support entailed a pronounced reorientation of the Lao P.D.R.'s trade, as the country was forced to look elsewhere for supplies of fuel and production inputs.

At the same time, rapid economic liberalization and growth in neighboring countries (in particular, China, Thailand, and Vietnam) provided ready markets for many products. These developments, together with the continued domestic economic decentralization and the improvements in infrastructure and border access (in particular, the completion in early 1994 of the first bridge across the Mekong, which provided an overland shipping route from Thailand to Vientiane), spurred large increases in recorded trade volume with the convertible area.

Exports to convertible markets more than tripled between 1990 and 1994 (Table 6).[16] Part of the increase was due to a considerable expansion in wood exports; while strict controls over wood harvesting continued to apply, sales of both logs and timber rose substantially with the authorization of logging in areas where large-scale hydroelectric projects, in particular the Nam Theun reservoir project, were begun. With respect to other agricultural exports, coffee exports declined, owing to the disappearance of markets in the former CMEA, and exports of fruits and vegetables grew rapidly, owing to the expansion of outlets in Thailand.

The bulk of the export expansion, however, was concentrated in the nontraditional manufacturing sector. From a very small level in 1989–90, and despite quantitative restrictions on imports of Lao garments into certain industrial markets, garment exports increased tenfold to about $50 million (one fifth of total exports) in 1993–94, as new, partly foreign-financed companies began operations.[17] In tandem with economic reforms in China and Vietnam, the Lao P.D.R. has developed a large-scale transit trade, consisting primarily of re-exports of assembled motorbikes and automobiles to these neighboring countries. Finally, "other" exports (mainly manufactures and semimanufactures) increased dramatically—the effect of virtually complete decentralization of production and trade activities, as well as rapidly rising foreign investment.

Following buoyant electricity exports in 1990 and 1991, receipts fell in 1992, owing to the lagged effects of a drought, before recovering in 1993–94. To augment the export potential, which is now constrained by the capacity of existing dams and the rapidly increasing domestic demand, several large hydroelectric investment projects are under way and should substantially increase total generating capacity in the next few years.

Total imports have also increased dramatically (Table 7). Increases in imports were fueled by rising exports, as well as by very high levels of foreign direct investment in 1993–94 (see Appendix II for further discussion); in addition, grants and project aid from industrial countries rose substantially, financing primarily inputs for infrastructural investment projects. Convertible area imports of fuel and ma-

---

[16]In 1992, the Lao P.D.R. moved to a customs-based reporting system, which improved the quality and coverage of the trade statistics; some portion of the increases recorded in 1992 is due to this improvement. Trade statistics were improved again in 1993, when reporting was introduced for a number of provincial border posts, yielding yet another sharp rise in recorded trade. (The sharp increases between 1990 and 1992 and again between 1992 and 1993 in the "other" trade category in Tables 6 and 7 are thus due in part to improved statistics.) Indeed, estimates indicate that both exports and imports may have been as much as 50 percent higher than officially recorded in 1990 and 1991, and as much as 20 percent higher in 1992. Thus, the sharp growth in recorded trade in the past few years may not have been as pronounced as indicated in Tables 6 and 7.

[17]Most raw materials for the industry were imported, and the contribution to value added is still only about 25 percent of export value.

Table 6. Composition of Exports

	1979	1980	1981	1982	1983	1984	1985	1986	1987	1988	1989	1990	1991	1992	Est. 1993	Est. 1994
Total exports	19.4	13.5	19.4	40.0	40.8	43.8	53.6	55.0	62.1	57.8	63.3	78.7	96.6	132.6	232.3	277.7
								(In millions of U.S. dollars)								
Convertible area	19.4	13.5	14.0	27.8	27.8	30.0	34.6	39.4	33.0	36.8	47.2	58.1	94.2	130.2	228.5	273.9
Wood and wood products	8.6	6.3	5.1	3.5	1.7	3.7	5.6	5.5	19.5	20.8	15.6	18.6	40.9	42.7	58.8	97.3
Coffee	4.1	1.1	—	—	1.6	0.6	0.3	2.1	0.9	0.5	3.6	1.4	2.2	2.4	3.3	3.3
Hydroelectric power	6.1	5.3	7.9	23.9	24.0	25.2	25.7	29.8	11.6	11.3	15.0	19.2	21.3	17.0	19.6	24.8
Garments	—	—	—	—	—	—	—	—	—	—	4.0	7.0	15.1	27.3	49.0	51.5
Re-exports	—	—	—	—	—	—	—	—	—	—	—	4.8	9.7	22.0	36.0	43.1
Other	0.5	0.8	1.0	0.4	0.5	0.5	3.0	2.0	1.0	4.2	9.0	7.1	5.0	18.8	61.8	53.9
Nonconvertible area	...	...	5.4	12.2	13.0	13.8	19.0	15.6	29.1	21.0	16.1	20.6	2.4	2.4	3.8	3.8
Coffee	...	...	...	8.1	6.9	8.1	8.2	7.1	8.5	6.8	5.2	7.2	0.9	...	...	...
Wood	...	...	...	0.5	1.3	1.3	5.6	2.3	13.4	9.3	5.8	7.3	0.8	...	...	...
Tin	...	...	...	1.0	1.1	1.3	1.1	2.8	1.9	2.1	2.2	1.3	0.2	...	...	...
Other	...	...	...	2.6	3.7	3.1	4.1	3.4	5.3	2.8	2.9	4.8	0.5	...	...	...
								(In percent of total exports)								
Total exports	100.0	100.0	100.0	100.0	100.0	100.0	100.0	100.0	100.0	100.0	100.0	100.0	100.0	100.0	100.0	100.0
Wood and wood products	44.3	46.7	26.3	10.0	7.4	11.4	20.9	14.2	53.0	52.1	33.8	32.9	43.2	32.2	25.3	35.0
Coffee	21.2	8.1	—	20.3	20.8	19.9	15.9	16.7	15.1	12.6	13.9	10.9	3.2	1.8	1.4	1.2
Electricity	31.6	39.3	40.7	59.8	58.8	57.5	47.9	54.2	18.7	19.6	23.7	24.4	22.0	12.8	8.4	8.9
Garments	—	—	—	—	—	—	—	—	—	—	6.2	8.9	15.6	20.6	21.1	18.5
Other (including re-exports)	2.8	5.9	33.0	10.0	13.0	11.2	15.3	14.9	13.2	15.7	22.4	22.9	15.9	32.6	43.7	36.3
Convertible area	...	...	72.2	69.5	68.1	68.5	64.6	71.6	53.1	63.7	74.6	73.8	97.5	98.2	98.4	98.6
Nonconvertible area	...	...	27.8	30.5	31.9	31.5	35.4	28.4	46.9	36.3	25.4	26.2	2.5	1.8	1.6	1.4

Sources: Lao authorities; and IMF staff estimates.

Table 7. Composition of Imports

	1979	1980	1981	1982	1983	1984	1985	1986	1987	1988	1989	1990	1991	1992	Est. 1993	Est. 1994
												(In millions of U.S. dollars)				
Total imports	70.3	92.3	90.2	132.2	149.4	161.9	193.1	185.7	216.2	162.4	210.7	201.6	215.0	265.6	410.7	528.0
Convertible area	28.3	50.0	48.2	73.7	76.3	59.3	77.5	78.4	81.7	90.4	135.6	130.7	210.4	265.6	410.7	528.0
Rice and foodstuffs	1.3	10.7	2.0	5.6	6.3	4.0	1.7	3.0	7.7	17.9	24.6	18.4	28.4	31.6	46.4	60.0
Petroleum products	8.8	12.9	12.9	13.8	14.0	10.8	10.6	7.8	6.4	6.3	12.2	7.3	21.1	24.3	29.5	41.7
Machinery and raw materials[1]	9.8	19.1	25.3	45.6	40.2	34.2	50.3	49.6	40.9	36.6	68.3	79.8	103.2	137.1	183.8	218.8
Imports for re-export	—	—	—	—	—	—	—	—	—	—	—	4.8	9.7	22.0	36.0	43.1
Other[2]	8.4	7.3	8.0	8.7	15.8	10.3	14.9	18.0	26.7	29.6	30.5	20.4	48.0	50.6	115.0	164.4
Nonconvertible area	42.0	42.3	42.0	58.5	73.1	102.6	115.6	107.3	134.5	72.0	75.1	70.9	4.6	—	—	—
												(In percent of total imports)				
Total imports	100.0	100.0	100.0	100.0	100.0	100.0	100.0	100.0	100.0	100.0	100.0	100.0	100.0	100.0	100.0	100.0
Convertible area	40.3	54.2	53.4	55.7	51.1	36.6	40.1	42.2	37.8	55.7	64.4	64.8	97.9	100.0	100.0	100.0
Rice and foodstuffs	1.8	11.6	2.2	4.2	4.2	2.5	0.9	1.6	3.6	11.0	11.7	9.1	13.2	11.9	11.3	11.4
Petroleum products	12.5	14.0	14.3	10.4	9.4	6.7	5.5	4.2	3.0	3.9	5.8	3.6	9.8	9.1	7.2	7.9
Machinery and raw materials	13.9	20.7	28.0	34.5	26.9	21.1	26.0	26.7	18.9	22.5	32.4	39.6	48.0	51.6	44.8	41.4
Imports for re-export	—	—	—	—	—	—	—	—	—	—	—	2.4	4.5	8.3	8.8	8.2
Other	11.9	7.9	8.9	6.6	10.6	6.4	7.7	9.7	12.4	18.2	14.5	10.1	22.3	19.1	28.0	31.1
Nonconvertible area	59.7	45.8	46.6	44.3	48.9	63.4	59.9	57.8	62.2	44.3	35.6	35.2	2.1	—	—	—

Sources: Lao authorities; and IMF staff estimates.

[1] Including unidentified tied-aid imports.

[2] Including private imports and small border trade.

Table 8. Composition of Services
(In millions of U.S. dollars)

	1988	1989	1990	1991	1992	Est. 1993	Est. 1994
Convertible area, net	5.0	7.1	13.6	−2.5	20.4	39.7	34.8
Receipts	18.2	23.3	25.9	40.0	63.3	85.9	95.1
Overflight	5.7	7.6	7.1	8.3	10.4	11.3	8.4
Embassies and international organizations	10.9	12.2	13.0	18.4	25.2	30.4	25.8
Transportation	0.5	1.0	1.0	2.5	4.1	3.1	2.9
Tourism	0.6	1.7	2.6	7.5	18.1	34.0	54.5
Factor payments	0.5	0.8	2.2	3.3	5.5	7.1	3.5
Payments	−13.2	−16.2	−12.3	−42.5	−42.9	−46.2	−60.3
Embassies and international organizations	−0.9	−0.7	−1.2	−4.5	−4.9	−5.0	−5.9
Transportation	−0.6	−2.8	−0.9	−5.8	−4.9	−6.0	−8.7
Private travel	...	...	...	−6.2	−9.7	−11.0	−18.0
Insurance services	...	...	...	−2.1	−3.2	−3.5	−5.4
Technical assistance	−9.2	−9.6	−7.0	−19.5	−15.8	−16.4	−16.5
Interest payments	−2.5	−3.1	−3.2	−4.4	−4.4	−4.3	−5.8
Nonconvertible area, net	−4.5	−2.6	−2.8	2.8	—	—	—
Services, net (convertible and nonconvertible areas)	0.5	4.5	10.8	−5.3	20.4	39.7	34.8

Sources: Lao authorities; and IMF staff estimates

chinery more than doubled between 1990 and 1994, not only because of a reallocation of demand away from the CMEA but also because of the strong growth in project financing and foreign direct investment. Even more impressive was the growth in imports of foodstuffs, consumer goods, and other manufactures, which more than tripled over the four-year period.

Finally, the nature of trade in services also changed significantly over the later reform period (Table 8). While inflows of technical assistance and receipts from embassies and international organizations remained an important part of services flows, tourism receipts increased twentyfold from 1990 to 1994; this rise was partially offset by greater travel abroad by Lao residents.

VI Fiscal Adjustment

The systemic reform, which accelerated following the introduction of the NEM in 1985, has dramatically changed the importance and operation of the budgetary process in the Lao P.D.R. With the emergence of a market economy, the budget has assumed a major role in bringing about macroeconomic stability by mobilizing domestic revenue, restraining expenditure, and channeling foreign assistance.

On the structural side, the tax system was overhauled to meet the needs of a nascent market economy; expenditures were prioritized; and fiscal management was enhanced by integrating central and provincial budgets into the national budget. However, major weaknesses still remained in the areas of tax administration, expenditure control, and public investment programming and execution.

Overall Fiscal Policy

Over the period 1988–94, public finance improved considerably, notably with the reduction of overall fiscal imbalances.[18] In particular, the current account balance swung from a deficit of 1 percent of GDP in 1988 to a surplus of almost 1 percent of GDP in 1993/94, facilitated by a combination of tax reform and current expenditure restraint. The ensuing public sector saving was utilized to finance increased capital spending. Thus, during 1988–94, the overall budget deficit (excluding grants) declined from nearly 20 percent of GDP to 11 percent of GDP (Table 9 and Chart 4).[19] During this period, the Government's dependence on external assistance remained at about 5 percent of GDP.

Initial Weakness of Fiscal Policy

Until 1989, when the SAF-supported program was put in place, fiscal policy had not been effective be-cause available information on the budget was insufficiently accurate, owing primarily to the severe underestimation of many of its components. Several factors contributed to this underestimation. First, the large exchange rate overvaluation understated government expenditures, particularly capital spending, which was mostly foreign financed.[20] Second, substantial subsidies (estimated at about 7 percent of GDP in 1987) on consumer goods purchased by civil servants were financed out of the profits of the Lao Food Corporation. Third, while the budget presentation did not show any direct recourse to credit from the domestic banking system, state enterprises had, in fact, borrowed heavily from the banking sector to help finance their compulsory transfers to the budget; this borrowing made the overall revenue performance of the Government appear rosier than it actually was while intensifying pressures on monetary aggregates. Fourth, debt-service payments did not reflect the payments made to the nonconvertible area, which amounted to about 1 percent of GDP in 1987.

The correction of fiscal imbalances was far from smooth during 1984–88, the period immediately preceding the adjustment and reform supported by the SAF arrangement. Revenue performance was initially weak, owing to a worsening of the financial position of state enterprises—which provided between two thirds and three fourths of total revenue—and a poor outturn of other taxes. Meanwhile, expenditures soared because of price and exchange rate adjustments and large wage increases. Later, in 1986–87, fiscal accounts improved significantly, reflecting substantial improvements in the financial position of enterprises following the price liberalization.

In 1988, however, the overall fiscal performance deteriorated sharply. While the tax reform of March 1988 contributed to a sharp increase in the ratio of revenue to GDP to some 12 percent, the ratio of expenditure to GDP more than doubled to 32 percent. This latter increase reflected the more than doubling

---

[18]This period also witnessed an increased transparency in the budgetary accounts following the adoption of market-based prices and exchange rates and the monetization of subsidies.

[19]As detailed later in this section, comparisons with earlier periods are biased by the use of an overvalued exchange rate.

[20]The impact of the exchange rate overvaluation on revenues was of minor importance because it affected only foreign exchange receipts by public enterprises, such as the state electricity company, and other minor items, such as overflight rights.

Table 9. General Government Budget

	1984	1985	1986	1987	1988	1989	1990	1991	1991/92[1]	1992/93	1993/94	1994/95
							(In billions of kip)					
Revenue	4.9	10.3	18.5	20.1	28.5	35.6	61.0	74.7	85.6	113.3	135.8	169.6
Tax	1.7	1.4	1.8	2.0	21.5	27.4	37.6	54.4	60.8	85.9	106.7	136.7
Nontax	3.3	8.9	16.7	18.1	7.1	8.1	23.3	20.3	24.9	27.3	29.1	32.9
Expenditure	8.3	19.6	26.5	29.5	75.0	106.4	143.4	151.1	174.4	170.5	258.9	290.8
Current	4.1	9.5	14.8	16.0	28.0	39.9	69.9	82.0	99.5	104.9	127.1	151.0
Without wages	(0.6)	(2.5)	(4.8)	(5.1)	(11.3)	(19.6)	(35.6)	(36.7)	(37.0)	(44.1)	(56.1)	(66.5)
Capital	4.3	10.2	11.7	13.5	47.0	66.5	73.6	69.1	74.9	65.6	131.8	140.0
Overall balance (commitment basis)	−3.4	−9.3	−8.0	−9.4	−46.5	−70.8	−82.5	−76.4	−88.7	−57.3	−123.1	−121.0
Arrears clearance (net)[2]	...	...	...	...	...	...	−5.9	−5.0	−6.8	−15.7	...	...
Overall balance (cash basis)	−3.4	−9.3	−8.0	−9.4	−46.5	−70.8	−88.4	−81.4	−95.6	−72.9	−123.1	−1211.0
Grants	1.5	2.0	1.7	1.2	12.6	16.9	23.0	32.6	34.0	31.3	67.3	52.5
Other foreign resources	2.1	7.5	6.6	8.4	32.6	66.0	60.3	29.6	47.2	27.1	50.6	58.0
Domestic financing	−0.1	−0.2	−0.2	−0.2	1.3	−12.1	5.1	19.3	14.3	14.5	5.2	10.5
							(In percent of GDP)					
Revenue	15.9	13.6	14.9	9.6	12.2	8.3	9.9	10.3	10.5	11.9	12.2	13.3
Tax	5.4	1.9	1.4	0.9	9.1	6.4	6.1	7.5	7.4	9.0	9.6	10.7
Nontax	10.5	11.8	13.5	8.7	3.0	1.9	3.8	2.8	3.0	2.9	2.6	2.6
Expenditure	27.0	26.0	21.3	14.1	32.0	24.9	23.4	20.9	21.4	17.9	23.2	22.8
Expenditure (exchange rate adjusted)	77.4	72.5	41.0	32.1	39.3	26.2	24.3	21.8	22.1	18.1	23.3	22.8
Current	13.3	12.5	11.9	7.6	11.9	9.4	11.4	11.3	12.2	11.0	11.4	11.8
Capital	13.7	13.5	9.4	6.4	20.0	15.6	12.0	9.6	9.2	6.9	11.8	10.9
Overall balance (cash basis; excluding grants)	−11.1	−12.4	−6.5	−4.5	−19.8	−16.6	−14.4	−11.3	−11.7	−7.8	−11.0	−9.5
Grants	4.8	2.6	1.3	0.6	5.4	4.0	3.7	4.5	4.2	3.3	6.0	4.1
Other foreign resources	6.6	10.0	5.3	−0.1	13.9	15.5	9.8	4.1	5.8	2.9	4.5	4.5
Domestic financing	−0.3	−0.2	−0.2	−0.1	0.6	−2.8	0.8	2.7	1.8	1.5	0.5	0.8
Current balance (excluding grants)	2.6	1.1	3.0	1.9	0.2	−1.0	−1.5	−1.0	−1.7	0.9	0.8	1.5

Source: Lao authorities.
[1]In 1992, the fiscal year was changed to October 1–September 30. 1991/92 (October–September) was included for purposes of comparison.
[2]Minus sign indicates net payment for clearing arrears.

of current and capital expenditures in 1988. The Government's adoption of a large wage increase in the public sector to replace food coupon payments following the price liberalization pushed current expenditure to almost 12 percent of GDP (compared with 8 percent of GDP in 1987). Meanwhile, the January 1988 devaluation of the official exchange rate—which was used to record government transactions—caused foreign-financed capital expenditure to increase sharply to about 20 percent of GDP from some 6 percent of GDP in 1987. Reflecting these developments, the overall budget deficit soared to 20 percent of GDP in 1988 from 5 percent of GDP in 1987 (Table 9 and Chart 4).

Fiscal Consolidation of 1989–1993/94

The fiscal situation improved significantly during 1989–1993/94,[21] as the Government pursued an adjustment policy under programs supported by the SAF and the ESAF. Total revenue recovered steadily from some 8 percent of GDP in 1989 to 12 percent of GDP in 1993/94. Concurrently, total expenditure in relation to GDP declined from about 25 percent in 1989 to some 23 percent in 1993/94.[22] As a result,

[21]In 1992, the fiscal year was changed to October 1–September 30.
[22]The 1993/94 expenditure figure had a strong upward bias, given the large carryovers of major projects from previous years.

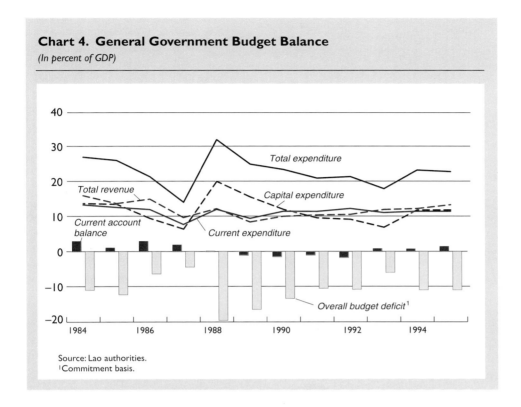

Chart 4. General Government Budget Balance
(In percent of GDP)

Source: Lao authorities.
[1]Commitment basis.

the current account balance recorded a surplus of 1 percent of GDP in 1993/94, a major turnaround from the persistent deficits in preceding years (Table 9 and Chart 4).

Tax Reform

The tax reform thus far has gone through two stages.[23] In the first stage, which culminated in a package of measures promulgated in March 1988, the reform aimed at correcting the most serious structural distortions stemming from the almost exclusive reliance on the practice of transferring operating surpluses of the public enterprises to the budget. In the second stage, which began in June 1989, the reform has corrected some earlier problems associated with the design of the new tax regime and introduced additional taxes in accordance with the needs of a market economy.

Reform of 1988

The crucial element of the March 1988 reform was the replacement of the state enterprises' trans-

fers to the budget by profit and turnover taxes. The profit tax was first levied on manufacturing enterprises with rates ranging from 20 percent to 85 percent while the turnover tax, with rates ranging from 1 percent to 15 percent, was levied on service enterprises.[24] The reform also included the introduction of taxes on export profits at rates varying from 50 percent to 80 percent. Finally, the maximum rate of the import tax was reduced from 200 percent to 70 percent, while its taxable base was revalued to reflect the exchange rate realignment. Following the reform, the share of tax revenue in total revenue rose from 9 percent during 1987–88 to 76 percent in 1988–89, and then to 79 percent in 1993/94 (see Table 10).

Reform of 1989

The June 1989 reform aimed at correcting some of the design problems arising from the 1988 reform and at making substantial progress toward a modern tax system. In place of the system of taxing gross income earned in individual export activities, specific export taxes on a limited number of natural resources (timber, wood products, animals, and certain scrap metals) were introduced, an ad valorem tax of

---

[23]In the coming years, the tax system is expected to be reformed further with IMF technical assistance.

[24]Both taxes were applied first only on domestic activity.

Table 10. Structure of Tax Revenue
(In percent)

	Share in Total Revenue						Share in GDP					
	Average 1984–85	Average 1986–87	Average 1988–89	Average 1990–93/94	1993/94	Budget 1994/95	Average 1984–85	Average 1986–87	Average 1988–89	Average 1990–93/94	1993/94	Budget 1994/95
Total revenue							14.8	12.2	10.2	11.0	12.2	13.3
Tax revenue	23.7	9.6	76.2	72.0	78.6	80.6	3.6	1.2	7.8	7.9	9.6	10.7
Profit tax	3.4	1.0	19.7	13.0	8.4	9.7	0.5	0.1	2.1	1.4	1.0	1.3
Income tax	0.2	0.1	0.1	3.0	5.3	5.0	—	—	—	0.3	0.6	0.7
Agriculture/land tax	3.5	2.2	4.0	2.0	1.6	2.1	0.5	0.3	0.4	0.2	0.2	0.3
Business licenses	0.1	0.1	0.1	0.5	0.1	0.1	—	—	—	—	—	—
Turnover tax	13.5	4.7	28.2	13.0	14.7	14.8	2.1	0.6	2.8	1.4	1.8	2.0
Of which:												
Public enterprises	6.6	2.9	21.3	—	—	—	1.0	0.4	2.2	—	—	—
Foreign trade tax	2.6	1.5	23.4	25.8	24.9	22.1	0.4	0.2	2.4	2.8	3.0	2.9
Import tax	2.1	1.2	17.3	14.6	18.9	18.0	0.3	0.1	1.8	1.6	2.3	2.4
Export tax	0.5	0.3	4.9	11.2	5.9	4.1	0.1	—	0.5	1.2	0.7	0.5
Excise tax	—	—	—	2.8	3.7	5.4	—	—	—	0.3	0.5	0.7
Timber royalties	—	—	—	7.3	15.5	17.1	—	—	—	0.9	1.9	2.3
Other	0.3	0.1	0.5	4.7	4.4	4.3	—	—	—	0.5	0.5	0.6
Nontax revenue	76.3	90.4	23.8	28.0	21.4	19.4	11.2	11.1	2.5	3.0	2.6	2.6
State enterprises	67.6	81.4	10.0	8.0	2.2	2.3	9.9	9.9	1.0	0.8	0.3	0.3
Other	8.7	9.0	13.8	20.0	19.2	17.1	1.3	1.1	1.4	2.2	2.3	2.3

Source: Lao authorities.

80 percent on electricity exports was imposed, and other export taxes were abolished.

With respect to the taxation of enterprises, the multiple corporate income tax rates were unified at 45 percent (except for the rate of 60 percent that continued to be applied to commercial bank profits), while the scope of the turnover tax was broadened by using five rates ranging from 3 percent to 20 percent to cover all services (excluding banking and insurance), wholesale trade, and imports. The personal income tax was extended to cover not only the wages and salaries of nationals employed by foreigners but also all salaried workers (including civil servants); the tax set no minimum threshold for taxable income while establishing a progressive tax schedule, with rates ranging from 2 percent to 30 percent. In addition, separate progressive income tax schedules were established for individuals engaged in industrial and commercial activities and for the self-employed, while taxes on agricultural income, rents, and dividends were lowered. Finally, specific ad valorem taxes were imposed on the domestic exploitation of natural resources to promote environmental conservation, and a land tax on the use of nonagricultural land was introduced.

A notable feature of the Lao tax system is that more than 50 percent of government revenues are collected through the enterprises (defined as public and private entities having a physical establishment, employing workers, and producing manufacturing and service activities). In particular, enterprises are subject to two alternative regimes of income declaration and tax imposition: (i) an "ordinary" imposition system, applied to enterprises with turnovers greater than KN 7.2 million a year; and (ii) a "negotiated" imposition system for other enterprises, which provides that a flat tax will be negotiated for taxpayers with unaudited accounts. Enterprises subject to the ordinary imposition system must comply with regular accounting standards and declare monthly turnovers and quarterly profits. This reporting is required not only to compute profit and turnover taxes but also to assess excise taxes on domestic sales and imports. The system is also used to assess income taxes on wage earners, based on the number and the type of workers employed by enterprises.

Reforms of the 1990s

Reforms in the 1990s aimed mainly at improving the structure of the system introduced in 1989. The following were the main additions and modifications:

- The turnover tax was simplified by reducing the number of rates from five to two (5 percent and 10 percent) in February 1991.

- Excise taxes were introduced on petroleum products and luxury goods in February 1991.

- A minimum corporate tax, levied at 1.5 percent of turnover, was established in February 1991 but implemented only in January 1993.

- A registration tax was introduced in September 1991.

- A land tax was introduced in December 1992 on agricultural and urban land, as a substitute for the agriculture tax.

- Timber royalties were restructured in October 1992.

- Export taxes were eliminated in June 1994.

- The import tariff system was restructured in January 1995.

Outstanding Issues

Despite the progress achieved so far in restructuring the tax system, revenue performance has remained weak; in addition, the revenue structure is inelastic, the tax base limited, and tax administration highly deficient. In 1993/94, total revenue was still very low, at about 12 percent of GDP, and relied mainly on indirect taxation (Table 10). The turnover and international trade taxes accounted for about 40 percent of total revenue (the largest share), followed by special taxes, such as timber royalties, which provided about 18 percent of total revenue. Taxes on personal and enterprise income accounted for about 5 percent of total revenue. The share of profit tax, which the 1989 reform had targeted as the tax providing the bulk of total tax revenue, actually declined from 17 percent of total revenue in 1989 to only 8 percent in 1993/94. Against the background of booming private sector activity, this decline clearly indicates widespread tax evasion and serious weaknesses in tax administration.

Low revenue buoyancy and skewed distribution appear to derive neither from flaws in the design of the tax system nor from a failure to introduce needed new taxes, such as a value-added tax (VAT).[25] Instead, the cause appears to be weak tax administration, ranging from a lack of control over the provincial authorities' collection procedures to an insufficient inspection of enterprises' tax declarations. Particularly weak is the administration of the turnover taxes on domestic activities and imports (see Box 4), the collection of which is based on the income declaration of enterprises. Although such a system can greatly facilitate tax collection, it is also

---

[25]The introduction of a VAT should be preceded by a substantial strengthening of the enterprise accounting standards, which is not foreseeable in the near future.

Box 4. Structure of Revenue Collection

The revenue structure of the Lao P.D.R. is characterized by the five principal sources of revenue.

Duties on international trade are collected by the Customs Department and in 1993/94 represented about 25 percent of total revenue. Import duties—which have only a mild protective component (see Box 3)—are collected at five regional customs posts, based on the valuation method of the General Agreement on Tariffs and Trade.[1] Import tariffs are ad valorem, and exemptions and rebates are clearly listed in the recently approved Customs Law. Export duties are currently applied only to exports of electricity in the amount of 20 percent of total sales and to a limited number of forestry products not covered by timber royalties.[2]

Taxes on domestic activities and imports are collected by the Tax Department based on enterprises' declarations. This category represented about 54 percent of total revenue in 1993/94 and comprises the following duties: (i) turnover tax and excise tax on imports; (ii) turnover tax and excise tax on domestic sales; (iii) profit tax; (iv) income tax (including taxes on wages,

_____

[1]The system is being gradually implemented. The past valuation method, based on official value estimates by product, may still be applied to some commodities.

[2]Other duties previously applied to selected agricultural products have recently been abolished.

cial authorities provided about 40 percent of the total revenue under this category.

capital earnings, and rental income); (v) registration tax and other taxes; and (vi) penalties. In 1993/94, provincal authorities provided about 40 percent of the total revenue under this category.

Land tax is collected by the Land Registration Department and provides only a small part of total revenue. The tax, which has recently replaced the agriculture tax, is levied in accordance with the use and location of the land (see Appendix IV for details).

Timber royalties are collected directly by the Budget Department through provincial authorities and represented about 15 percent of total revenue in 1993/94. The amount of royalties is determined in accordance with the quality of wood exported while the total amount of cut wood is determined by an annual nationwide plan. Although recent legislation has regulated new logging permits, the main outstanding issue remains the sustainability of this source of revenue in the medium term, when the exploitation of hydroelectric project areas—which represents the only major source of new logging now being allowed—will be exhausted. In particular, it is still unclear whether royalties on the exploitation of other natural resources, especially lignite, will be able to make up for the expected decrease in timber royalties.

Nontax revenue is collected at the central level by the State Assets Department (which collects leasing income from privatized state enterprises, concessions, and dividends and other payments from state-owned enterprises) and the Budget Department itself. In 1993/94, nontax revenue represented about 21 percent of total revenue.

---

open to tax evasion unless an appropriate system of cross verification is put in place. Indeed, in the Lao P.D.R., tax verifications and controls are extremely loose; the tax department is severely understaffed; declarations are hardly examined; payment arrears are not pursued; and on-the-spot inspections are rare and ineffective. In addition, because the enterprise accounting system is not widely enforced, too many firms still adhere to simplified accounting, even though their turnover is well beyond the KN 7.2 million threshold. These firms are, therefore, subject not to the ordinary but to the negotiated imposition system, which encourages collusion between taxpayers and tax officers and causes large revenue losses for the Government.

Similar problems—particularly understaffing and, hence, the lack of enforcement—affect the administration of all other taxes. In the case of the land tax, the lack of personnel is compounded by the absence of land titles and registration, which erodes the tax base. Meanwhile, in the provinces, tax collection is made difficult by limited monetization.

Expenditure and Fiscal Management

Improved control of spending was an important element of recent fiscal adjustment. However, the observed changes in expenditure composition would suggest that both recurrent and capital expenditure have not yet been managed in a manner fully consistent with established priorities and long-term planning.

Expenditure Trends

Two major trends have emerged in the expenditure composition. The first is a sharp relative decline in capital expenditure. Public investment dropped continuously from 13.6 percent of GDP in the 1984–85 period to 7 percent of GDP in 1992/93, before recovering to 11 percent of GDP in 1993/94. One reason for this trend is that, as the privatization of state enterprises progressed during the early 1990s, investment activities previously performed by the Central Government were transferred to the

Chart 5. Structure of Government Expenditure

(In percent)

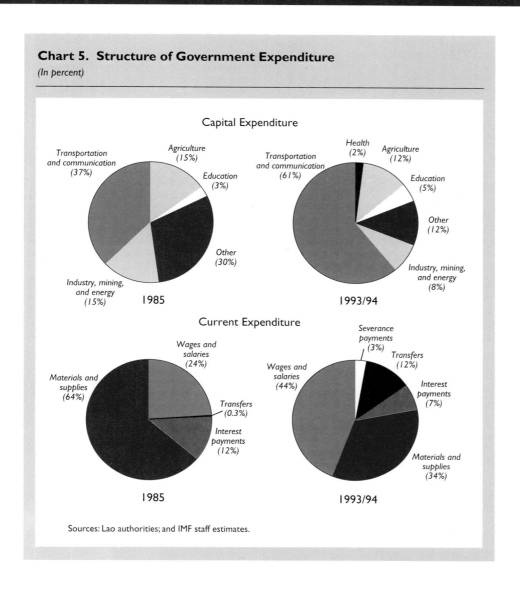

Capital Expenditure

1985

1993/94

Current Expenditure

1985

1993/94

Sources: Lao authorities; and IMF staff estimates.

private sector.[26] The second reason is related to the increasing problems with absorptive capacity, as evidenced by the substantial accumulation of undisbursed foreign financing in the past few years. Be-

[26]The Government henceforth concentrated on infrastructure expenditure rather than on directly productive activities. This shift is reflected in the increased share of public expenditure in the transportation and communications sector (61 percent of the total in 1993/94, compared with 37 percent in 1985, as shown in Chart 5), and in the corresponding decline of the share of the industry, mining, and energy sector (from 15 percent in 1985 to 8 percent in 1993/94). Among the recently emerging sectors are education, with a 5 percent share in 1993/94, compared with 3 percent in 1985, and health, with about a 2 percent share, compared with a virtually nonexistent share in 1985. These shares, however, remain rather low by international standards if measured in terms of GDP, particularly in view of the very low social indicators of the Lao P.D.R.

cause the authorities lacked an effective system of public investment prioritization and monitoring (see below), more public investments were initiated than could actually be implemented. A slowdown in project implementation across the board ensued, causing widespread cost overruns.

The second trend is that the composition of current expenditure has changed markedly in favor of workers' compensation—defined as wages and salaries, and transfers and severance payments. The share of workers' compensation rose from 24 percent of current expenditure in 1985 to 44 percent in 1993/94 (see Chart 5), while current expenditure remained virtually unchanged in terms of GDP. This trend has both a positive and a negative aspect. The positive aspect is that fringe benefits and food subsidies, previously hidden, have been gradually either monetized or expressly recorded as workers' compensation,[27] resulting in a more transparent budget. The negative aspect is that the increased share of workers' compensation corresponded to a declining share of materials and supplies, which dropped sharply from 64 percent in 1985 to 34 percent in 1993/94 (Chart 5). This fall adversely affected the necessary operation and maintenance of the existing limited infrastructure.

Progress in Fiscal Management

The progress that has been made in strengthening fiscal management can be summarized as follows.

First, to increase budget discipline, the Government discontinued its decentralization policy and reverted to fiscal centralization in August 1991. Provincial administrations ceased to run independent budgets, and central government and provincial budgets were consolidated into a single budget document, the finalization of which is subject to guidelines and clearance by the Council of Ministers before its approval by the National Assembly. In 1992, a national budget, covering all revenues and expenditures of the Central Government and the 17 provincial administrations, was prepared for the first time since 1975.

Second, new budgetary decrees were implemented in early 1993 to streamline budgetary procedures and to conform with the centralization of the budget and the new fiscal year (October–September). Moreover, with the enactment of a new budget law in June 1994, the steps of annual budget preparation were clearly defined, although the new nomenclature for budgetary accounts has yet to be adopted.

Third, budget execution was also centralized, and a new treasury system was established, replacing the previous system of disbursements made at the local level by the provincial branches of the central bank. In the new system, provincial authorities act under the general authority of, and as agents for, the Central Government in the collection of revenues and execution of expenditures. Provincial treasury offices have been established in the principal provinces (eight as of mid-1995) and eventually will be extended to all provinces to coordinate tax collections and payments at the local level.

Fourth, new accounting rules based on the standard double-entry system were introduced nationwide in July 1994. This new accounting framework has been established to attain an accurate recording of state operations and eventually to increase the re-

liability of general budgetary accounts for policy-making purposes.

Fifth, to improve capital expenditure planning, the multiyear rolling public investment plan has recently been revised, and a public investment management unit is being strengthened under a United Nations Development Program-sponsored project.

Outstanding Issues

Despite the progress achieved thus far, the annual budgetary formulation—from the initial preparation in the line ministries to its finalization at the National Assembly—as well as its execution and control is still in a trial phase. Budget allocation requests by line ministries are largely made by adjusting past expenditure patterns on an incremental basis, with no due regard paid to overall planning. Budget execution, including expenditure monitoring and control, is still somewhat inefficient as the treasury network has yet to be fully established. Finally, budgetary accounts still lack transparency, as budget classifications need to be more standardized and the quality and timeliness of data reporting require improvement.

Over the longer run, the lack of adequate medium-term fiscal planning capacity is one of the major weaknesses of fiscal management. Thus, despite the existence of a five-year public investment framework, the annual budget process hardly reflects medium-term guidelines.

In the absence of a reliable system for monitoring expenditures, the Lao authorities exert limited control. In practice, expenditure control is based on the cash position of the Treasury, as information on the expenditure program becomes available only with a long lag and is too scattered to be taken into account during the ongoing fiscal year. In addition, because line ministries can still exercise some discretion in managing public expenditures, misappropriations of funds and expenditure overruns are frequent.

Civil Service Reform

In late 1989, the Government embarked upon a thorough restructuring of the civil service as part of the process of moving toward a market-based economy. This process continued during 1990–93, with the reform focusing mainly on a reduction of non-military personnel, where numbers had swollen in the late 1980s to over 100,000 persons.[28] Beginning in March 1994, the retrenchment was accompanied by an overhaul of the salary structure in accordance

---

[27]For instance, some payments in kind to workers previously recorded among materials and supplies were transferred to wages and salaries in 1992/93.

[28]There are no firm figures on military personnel in the late 1980s.

Box 5. The Salary Reform of April 1994

In April 1994, the Lao Government introduced a revised pay structure for the civil service that was put into effect retroactively from March 1994. The objective was to improve the quality of public administration through a pay structure that rewards good performers and is competitive with that of the private sector.

The salary structure was revised upward for each job category. On average, by weighing the salary by the new personnel distribution among job categories (see below), the average base salary for the whole civil service rose by about 60 percent (by 83 percent for nonmilitary personnel, and by about 43 percent for military personnel).

All existing benefits and allowances (with the exception of children's allowances) were increased, and new benefits and allowances were introduced. On an annual basis, the budgetary cost of benefits and allowances more than doubled from KN 8.6 billion (about 0.8 percent of GDP) before April 1994 to KN 17.4 billion (about 1.6 percent of GDP) after April 1994.

Nonmilitary civil servants were reclassified into the five existing categories (with 15 steps each) according to academic and professional qualifications. The reclassification implied a drastic reduction in the share of personnel in the highest-paid categories, categories 5 and 4, from 7 percent and 17 percent of the total, respectively, to less than 1 percent and 11 percent, respectively, and a higher concentration at the lower end of the salary scale (categories 2 and 1).

In 1993/94, the number of nonmilitary personnel was reduced by about 3,700 (about 5 percent) on a net basis. At the end of September 1994, total nonmilitary personnel were estimated at about 69,000 persons. Furthermore, based on information on severance payments and the approximate magnitude of average payments to retrenched military workers, military personnel may have been retrenched by about 3,000 during 1993/94.

The overall impact of the new salary structure and the civil service reform on the 1993/94 budget was limited. In particular, wages and salaries (including base salaries and benefits) rose by about 27 percent, from KN 44.1 billion (4.7 percent of GDP) in 1992/93 to KN 56.1 billion (5 percent of GDP) in 1993/94. Over the same period, transfers (which include pensions, allowances, and contingencies) increased by about 24 percent from KN 12.6 billion (1.3 percent of GDP) to KN 15.6 billion (1.4 percent of GDP).

The budgetary impact of these increases was dampened by four major factors. First, the retrenchment of nonmilitary civil service personnel by some 5 percent resulted in a savings equivalent to about 10 percent of the wage bill under the old salary scale. Second, the savings derived from the retrenchment of military personnel was nearly as significant as that derived from the retrenchment of nonmilitary civil servants. Third, the reclassification of civil servants implied a downgrading of most personnel. Fourth, the increased salary structure was in effect only for the last seven months of the fiscal year 1993/94.

with qualifications and performance. The objective of this reform was to attain a pay structure competitive with that of the private sector, which eventually could enable the Government to reward good performers, retain well-qualified personnel, and improve the quality of public service. The results of the reform were encouraging: the number of nonmilitary personnel dropped by about 23 percent between 1989 and 1994, while the budget cost for total workers' compensation was contained to about 6 percent of GDP in 1992/93 and 1993/94.

Reform of 1989

The civil service reform was initiated in 1989 for two main reasons. First, administrators trained under the former centrally planned economic system were unable to keep up with the needs of a market-oriented economy. As a result, staff redundancies were evident in some areas, while there was a lack of qualified personnel and a high need for retraining in others. Second, the civil service staff was too large, given the need to reduce state control of the economy.

During the early stage, the reform succeeded in drastically reducing personnel across the board, as an estimated 19 percent of all civil service employees were retrenched between 1989 and 1992.

Reform of 1994

In March 1994, the retrenchment program was modified, as new legislation substantially changed pay structures and job classifications (see Box 5). The reform encompassed three main elements: (i) a restructuring of job classifications according to professional and academic experience, which implied, on average, a downgrading of existing personnel; (ii) a large upward revision of the salary scale in accordance with the new job classifications; and (iii) the further net retrenchment of about 3,500 persons in 1994.

Despite the sizable increase in average pay of about 80 percent, the budgetary impact of the reform was contained by the overhaul of job classifications, which called for a drastic drop in the share of personnel in the highest-paid categories, and by the net retrenchment. As a result, workers' compensation, including wages and salaries and transfers (pensions, allowances, and contingencies), rose from about 6 percent in 1992/93 to only 6.4 percent of GDP in 1993/94.[29] To maintain fiscal discipline in the medium term, the Government is expected to limit hiring strictly and continue the retrenchment of personnel. To this end, it will strengthen the monitoring of civil service reform, particularly by establishing a specific monitoring unit at the Ministry of Finance to record the hiring, retrenchment, and reallocation of civil servants.

---

[29]Budget costs were limited also because the reform, coming at midyear, had only a seven-month impact on the 1993/94 budget.

VII Privatization and State Enterprise Reform

In the late 1980s, the Government, responding to increasing concerns about the weak performance of the state-owned enterprises, began to formulate a strategy for privatization and state enterprise reform. At first, during 1988–90, the emphasis was on granting greater managerial autonomy to state-owned enterprises, and the privatization program was limited mainly to small enterprises. Starting in March 1991, the program's emphasis shifted to include more of the larger enterprises, and a more articulate plan was announced whereby all but a handful of "strategic enterprises" had to be privatized within three years.

Overall, the privatization program, although slower in developing than originally envisaged, was quite successful; out of some 200 centrally managed enterprises existing in 1989, 65 were privatized by December 1994. However, the excessive reliance on leasing—as opposed to selling or hire purchasing—enterprises may need to be corrected to encourage longer-term investments and reduce the burden of administering such contracts.

State Enterprises Before 1990

At the end of 1989, the state enterprise sector comprised about 640 enterprises and accounted for virtually all the modern industrial sector.[30] State enterprises employed an estimated 16,000 workers (about 10 percent of the nonagricultural labor force). About two thirds of these enterprises—mainly the largest—were centrally managed, while the rest were managed by provincial and district authorities. Three fourths of the state enterprises were engaged in manufacturing, and the others in construction, electricity, and mining.

Prior to the introduction of the NEM in 1985, enterprises had no operating autonomy; they obtained allocations from the budget for their working capital, investment outlays, bonus payments, and welfare expenditures. In turn, as mentioned above, they were obliged to transfer to the budget all of their operating surpluses and to reimburse loans that they received from the Government for their fixed investment.[31]

In March 1988, the Government granted operating autonomy to state enterprises. Most of these—including the largest—became free to determine their production levels, wage and price policies, and investment plans. Subsidies and capital transfers to state enterprises were discontinued. In that connection, several state enterprises in 1989 substantially increased wages in cash for their employees, breaking with the previous system, under which they mainly issued payments in kind (with rice coupons) and then financed the losses with bank credit. Although the old system ceased in 1990, several state enterprises had already accumulated substantial overdue debts to the banking system.

Strategy for Privatization

The March 1988 decree on privatization clearly aimed at reducing the role of the Government in production and strengthening private sector activity. That decree, however, made no mention of criteria for privatization, such as the selection of firms to privatize, asset valuation procedures, and bidding standards. It was only in late 1990 that the exercise became more systematic. The enterprises to be privatized had to be ranked on the basis of the following criteria: (i) cost to the budget; (ii) need for capital; (iii) scope for attracting investors; and (iv) ability of workers to manage or own, or both, the enterprises. In practice, a number of other factors were also important: the size of the enterprises (smaller ones were preferred); the ability to conduct an acceptable valuation;[32] and the expected employment impact.

---

[30]There were also many smaller nonindustrial enterprises, for example, in the transportation, wholesale, and external trade sectors. The total number of these enterprises is not known with certainty.

[31]These reimbursements were made under the provisions of "depreciation allowances" under nontax revenues in the government budget.

[32]The valuation process has concentrated on assets rather than the income-generating potential of state-owned enterprises.

While a list of enterprises to be retained in the public sector has yet to be published, the Government outlined the broad criteria for this selection. According to Article 2 of Decree No. 17, enterprises "to be kept under state control are those having importance to the national economy, society, defense, and internal security." The decree specifies as strategic areas "electricity generation and distribution, waterworks, post and telecommunications, pharmaceuticals, domestic and international commercial airline flights, banking and insurance, the bulk purchase and sale consortium, mining of ore resources, logging, and the national defense industries."[33] However, owing to the lack of public capital, recent privatizations have included areas previously considered strategic, namely, road and bridge management and hydroelectricity. Indeed, the Government is considering allowing private participation in all areas of interest to the private sector except forestry and defense.

Results of the Privatization Program

Between the start of the privatization program in 1989 and December 1994, 64 centrally managed state enterprises were privatized out of a total of about 130. (See Table 11 for data on the privatization of centrally managed enterprises.)[34] The number of privatized enterprises grew each year between 1989 and 1992 before leveling off in 1993 and 1994. During 1989–92, 39 enterprises were privatized, with a total value of $41.4 million; during 1993–94, 25 additional enterprises were privatized, with a total value of $26.8 million. The number and value of privatized enterprises declined in the past two years because the most attractive and important investment opportunities had already been offered in response to strong demand by foreign investors.

Of the 58 privatized enterprises with data on the mode of privatization, 78 percent were leased, 19 percent sold (outright), and 3 percent hire purchased.[35] The average value of leased state enterprises (about $40,000) was higher than that for those sold (about $23,000) or hire purchased (about $3,000). Overall, for the 50 firms with data on the origin of investors, 42 percent of them were divested to domestic investors, 26 percent to joint ventures, and 32 percent to foreign investors. The average

value of state enterprises privatized through joint ventures (about $28,000) was higher than the average value of those that were fully sold to foreign investors (about $18,000) or domestic investors (about $4,000).

Before privatization, the 28 state enterprises with employment data employed 3,459 workers; immediately after privatization, employment fell to 3,029, as 14 percent of the workers were made redundant.[36] However, evidence from a recent urban labor force survey suggests that the unemployment impact was minor. Only 2.6 percent of the total urban labor force of almost 200,000 was unemployed in July 1992.

Data on the privatization program also indicate that the average size of the workforce taken over by foreign investors and joint ventures was significantly larger than that if the workforce taken over by domestic investors. Interestingly, job losses were lower for firms divested to foreign investors, possibly suggesting that foreign investors were less knowledgeable about individual skill levels, better able financially to bear excess employment, and more pressed by the Government to absorb excess labor.

While results of the privatization process at the provincial level are hard to gauge owing to the lack of adequate data, it appears that progress has been about as rapid as that at the central level in terms of the number of enterprises privatized. Sales of state enterprises, rather than leasing, dominated at the provincial level. At least 52 provincially managed enterprises were sold between 1988 and mid-1993, and at least 29 were leased.[37] The prevalence of selling as the mode of privatization reflects, among other things, the fewer legal restrictions on the sale of state assets at the provincial level than at the central level. The average value of enterprises privatized at this level was much smaller, mainly because of the lower average value of provincially managed state enterprises in general.

Although line ministries were central to the privatization process, they did not have direct responsibility for supervising the process. Before February 1992, responsibility for the privatization program lay with the New Economic Mechanism Financial Committee, headed by the Ministry of Economy, Planning and Finance.[38] In February 1992, the responsibility for formulating the program was transferred to the Privatization Committee of

---

[33]Notwithstanding the inclusion of banking in this list, the authorities allowed six new private commercial banks to start operations in 1993.

[34]Because of data problems, this discussion of results is limited to centrally managed state enterprises.

[35]Hire purchase denotes an agreement whereby the purchase price for an enterprise is paid in installments.

[36]This figure reflects only the initial employment impact of privatization; data on subsequent job losses are unavailable.

[37]The total number of provincially managed state enterprises is not available.

[38]The Ministry of Economy, Planning and Finance was split into the Ministry of Finance and the Committee for Planning and Cooperation in 1992.

Table 11. Privatization of Centrally Managed State-Owned Enterprises[1]

Enterprise Name and Year Privatized	Mode of Privatization			Contract			Number of Employees		
	Lease	Hire purchase	Sale	Origin of investor	Period (in years)	Value (in thousands of U.S. dollars)	Total	Retained	Dismissed
1989									
Sheet metal factory	x			...	15	175	...	...	...
Tobacco factory	x			...	5	14,000	1,037	939	98
1990									
Tha Ngone Mechanical Workshop No. 1	x			Domestic	10	50	...	...	...
Dong Doh Poultry Farm	x			Domestic	10	151	26	26	...
First of May Sawmill	x			Foreign	10	1,820	211	149	62
1991									
Rattan and bamboo factory	x			Domestic	10	216	31	19	12
Lao Plywood Factory	x			Foreign	15	8,400	378	349	29
Wood Product Factory No. 2	x			Foreign	15	620	236	230	6
Irrigation Pump Repair Workshop at Km 14	x			Foreign	10	121	20	20	...
Lao-Czech Pig Farm at Km 18	x			Domestic	10	57	18	18	...
Lao-Swedish Mechanical Workshop	x			Foreign	15	473	107	107	...
Tha Ngone Fish Farm	x			Domestic	10	109	...	...	...
Veune Kham Agriculture Technical Service Center	x			Domestic	5	78	41	40	1
Parquet Factory No. 1 at Km 14	x			Domestic	10	2,245	...	...	...
Wood Product Factory No. 1	x			Foreign	10	1,055	...	...	...
Paske People's Building				Domestic	20	200	...	...	...
Inter-Lao Tourism			x	Joint	...	65	...	...	...
1992									
Lao-Hungarian Poultry Farm [2]	x			...	2	22	...	...	...
Thanaleng Warehouse and Ferry	x			Foreign	15	2,678	122	100	22
Latkhouay Pig Farm	x			Domestic	20	241	27	27	—
Lao-Cuban Poultry Farm	x			Domestic	5	32	27	26	1
Tha Ngane Agriculture Mechanical Workshop	x			Domestic	5	28	44	44	—
Car Rental Company No. 1	x			...	15	79	87	40	47
Car Rental Company No. 2			x	Domestic	15	21	...	...	...
Champassak People's Building	x			...	20	400	...	...	...
Praksab Sugar Factory		x		Domestic	15	3,200	31	31	—
Savannakhet Building			x	...	60	...	...	...	...
Nabong Cattle Breeding	x			Joint	20	309	33	33	—
Electrical wire and plastic bag factory	x			Foreign	15	253	81	79	2
Detergent factory	x			Foreign	15	763	81	81	—
Tha Ngare Vegetable Center	x			Foreign	20	108	...	...	...
Phou Vao Hotel at Luang Prabang	x			Joint	35	700	...	...	...
Na Phank Seed Production Center	x			Foreign	20	232	...	...	...
Animal feed factory	x			Domestic	15	523	89	89	—
Baby food factory	x			Domestic	15	31	...	...	...
Tha Ngone Ferry	x			Domestic	5	115	6	6	—
Lao-Australian Heavy Mechanical Workshop at Tha Ngone	x			Joint	...	1,530	110	110	—
Borikharnsay Sawmill	x			Foreign	15	540	30	30	—
Lane Xang Hotel			x	Joint	...	3,500	...	...	...
1993									
Lao Brewery			x	Joint	...	10,200	197	197	—
Sikhay Sawmill	x			Foreign	15	346	92	65	27
Parquet Factory No. 2 at Km 14	x			Joint	15	2,263	190	67	123
Tannery factory, prefecture	x			Joint	25	1,250	...	...	...

Table 11 *(concluded)*

Enterprise Name and Year Privatized	Mode of Privatization			Contract			Number of Employees		
	Lease	Hire purchase	Sale	Origin of investor	Period (in years)	Value (in thousands of U.S. dollars)	Total	Retained	Dismissed
Pancheng Sugar Factory		x		Foreign	35	125	...	...	...
Phonehang Production									
Unit at Km 62	x			Domestic	20	123	...	...	...
Phousy Hotel, Luang Prabang	x			Joint	30	252	...	...	...
That Khoa Garment Factory	x			Domestic	15	63	...	...	...
Lao Soft Drink Company			x	Joint	...	2,380	107	107	—
Cultural Product Factory									
(wood sculpture)	x			Domestic	20	42	...	...	...
Muang Lao Hotel	x			Foreign	30	881	...	...	...
Lao Textile Factory									
of the Women's Federation			x	Joint	30	4,500	...	...	...
Garment Factory No. 1				...	...	...	...	...	...
Pharmaceutical factory			x	Foreign	...	...	...	...	...
1994									
Lao-Russian Workshop									
at Dang Chong	x			Domestic	10	665	...	...	...
Expert Service Building	x			Joint	30	1,350	...	...	...
Lao-Hungarian Poultry Farm[2]	x			Domestic	10	...	...	...	...
Building Construction No. 2		x		...	5	215	...	...	...
Building Construction No. 3		x		...	5	85	...	...	...
Laovieng Textile Factory,									
prefecture		x		Joint	40	150	...	...	...
Construction Company No. 2				...	...	1,035	...	...	...
Agricultural Transport Company				...	10	62	...	...	...
Agricultural machinery				...	...	11	...	...	...
Forestry Enterprise No. 2				...	...	83	...	...	...
Autotransport No. 1	x			Domestic	...	735	...	...	...
Total of privatized enterprises	64					68,249[3]	3,459[3]	3,029[3]	430[3]

Sources: Lao authorities; the World Bank; the Asian Development Bank; and IMF staff estimates.

[1]As of December 1994.

[2]This enterprise was first privatized in 1992. The lease was renewed in 1994.

[3]Total for enterprises for which data are available.

the Committee for Planning and Cooperation (CPC), and the responsibility for executing the CPC's decisions was assigned to the Permanent Office of the Privatization Committee (POPC) in March 1993.[39] However, owing to the lack of resources and information, the executing agency delegated to the line ministries the tasks of identifying, classifying, valuing, and prioritizing enterprises for privatization, with the executing agency merely supervising the process. Line ministries also recommended the mode of privatization and often identified potential transferees.

---

[39]The POPC was established at the headquarters of the CPC, with the Chairman of the CPC (who is also the Deputy Prime Minister) overseeing its activities and those of the POPC.

Problems with Privatization and Remedial Actions

Despite the overall success of the privatization process, several problems emerged in its methodology. The most important of these problems were the prevalence of leasing; weak accounting practices; the insufficiency of resources for the POPC; the lack of clear ranking criteria; and, more generally, the obscurity of the privatization process.

Prevalence of Leasing

The prevalence of fixed-term leasing was the major problem with the privatization process. Leasing has emerged as the main mode of privatization, reflecting the Government's reluctance to part completely with state enterprises and the legal prohibition of the selling of state land. In addition, leasing has been probably more politically acceptable than selling outright because of the public concern that the nation's holdings will be entirely sold. Furthermore, because of uncertainty about the value of state enterprises and the permanence of the economic reforms, the private sector may have preferred the less risky option of leasing rather than buying. Joint ventures were chosen as leasing agents when state enterprises were relatively large or required more sophisticated technology than the Lao public and private sectors were able to provide. Contracting out or leasing to workers' collectives was chosen when alternative modes of privatization were not practical.

Overrelying on leasing does, however, cause problems. Leasing does not change the ownership structure; it merely changes the management structure—and then only for a limited period. Because ownership is unchanged, leasing does not appear to stimulate investment. Indeed, leasing tends to encourage decapitalization because, with an average leasing length of 15 years, the owners have a limited horizon. Moreover, government monitoring of the leased state enterprises is costly and difficult. More recently, government policy has started to favor the sale of state enterprises, as buyers are being sought for expiring lease contracts.

Weak Accounting Practices

Weak accounting practices have also hindered the program. State enterprises lack reliable data on financial history, net worth, and profitability. Many of them have only recently (since 1990) started using international accounting methods, rather than the "unified" system prevalent in centrally planned economies. Similarly, enterprises offered for privatization are not independently audited, a factor that has adversely affected the private sector's confidence in the privatization process. Against this background, a system of regular, independent audits of state enterprises is being carried out by qualified personnel according to international accounting standards.

Insufficiency of POPC Resources

The POPC was not adequately staffed to perform its extensive privatization responsibilities. The POPC has a staff of only 14, even though it is responsible for coordinating the process, which includes surveying, valuing, prioritizing the privatization of enterprises, and finding bidders. The authorities plan to dedicate more resources and training to this effort, including through external technical assistance. In addition, given its limited resources, the POPC plans to concentrate on privatizing the larger (in terms of financial assets) enterprises.

Lack of Clear Ranking Criteria

As previously noted, the lack of clear ranking criteria for state-owned enterprises has hampered privatization, allowing line ministries to prioritize for privatization according to ministerial, rather than governmental, objectives.[40] A clear set of criteria is being established for the Government as a whole, and the POPC will rank all centrally managed state enterprises accordingly. These criteria will focus on the availability of a recent independent audit; the ability to establish a clear and definitive legal separation from the state; the size of the state enterprise (in general, larger ones should be given higher priority); and the expected demand from private sector investors.

Obscurity of Privatization Process

Public knowledge of the privatization program has been limited, and the overall process has been rather opaque. Information on the enterprises to be privatized has been scarce, although, invitations to bid should have been widely disseminated by decree, using newspapers, radio, and official bulletins. Indeed, the authorities have tended to favor direct contact with potential bidders rather than depend on costly and time-consuming publicity. In these circumstances, the public is not aware of the Government's privatization plans, the enterprises that are being considered for privatization, or the worth of these enterprises. To enhance the transparency of the privatization process and encourage wider private sector interest, a list of enterprises to be privatized and those to remain in the public sector has recently been promulgated.

Conclusion

Substantial progress has been made with the privatization program in the Lao P.D.R. Many enterprises of varying sizes and activity have been privatized without significant adverse impact on employment. Foreign interest has been significant, and the privatization process has been central to the economic liberalization program. However, improvements in the method of privatization could make the program more successful. In this connection, it should be emphasized that competitive, transparent, and well-defined procedures should be used throughout the privatization process.

---

[40]Nevertheless, if the POPC and the line ministries disagree on the selection of enterprises for privatization, the Cabinet makes the decision.

VIII   Past Reforms and Future Challenges

Assessment of Past Reforms

Overall, the reform efforts of the Lao Government from the mid-1980s to 1994 resulted in considerable progress in both systemic transformation and macroeconomic management. The basic elements of a market-oriented economic system are now in place, including (i) a market-based price system; (ii) a small but dynamic private sector; (iii) a two-tier banking system; and (iv) a broadly open foreign trade regime. As for macroeconomic management, the Government succeeded in reducing inflation sharply in the late 1980s and limiting it to a moderate rate in the early 1990s. This success was followed by improved output growth and a strengthened external position.

This is not to say that the reform process was without problems. There were many performance shortfalls: reform measures in the areas of taxation, privatization, and the civil service, as well as the updating of the rolling public investment plan, were not implemented fully as planned. Some delays were also experienced with regard to institution building, notably the establishment of a Treasury with an effective accounting system and the enactment of business and other laws. In some instances (such as privatization and civil service reform), the shortfalls partly reflected the overly ambitious targets in terms of both the scale and speed of reform. In most cases, however, political constraints and institutional and technical weaknesses combined to hamper effective implementation. Furthermore, structural reforms of this type are typically more difficult to achieve, in view of their greater political and social sensitivity and more demanding administrative and technical requirements, than other policy objectives. These factors—rather than any wavering in the authorities' commitment to the reform process—seemed primarily to account for the slippages in implementation.

Factors Facilitating Reform

The following factors favorably influenced the reform process.

- The Lao authorities' success in achieving macroeconomic stabilization during 1989–94 owed much to (i) the strong emphasis on demand management and the overall macroeconomic framework that was put in place, even though macroeconomic management lacked many of the indirect tools conventionally employed in a market economy; and (ii) the promptness with which the anti-inflationary policies were undertaken.
- The Lao economy was dominated by agriculture, not by industrial state-owned enterprises. These conditions facilitated the supply response to structural reforms and limited the possible adverse impact of state enterprise reform.
- Unlike other members of the former CMEA, the Lao P.D.R. did not have very extensive economic ties with the former Soviet Union. The country could therefore withstand the external shock during 1990–91 from the loss of aid (equivalent to about 4 percent of GDP) from the former Soviet Union and the loss of preferential trading arrangements with the countries of the former CMEA during 1990–91. Even so, some adverse impact would still have resulted from the shock were it not for two additional factors. First, the structural reform program had been introduced before Soviet aid was cut. Second, this aid cut was more than compensated for by a large increase in assistance from other bilateral and multilateral sources.
- Central planning was not deeply entrenched in the Lao economy. Because central planning had been introduced only in 1975 and even then in a hesitant and somewhat ad hoc manner, collectivization and centralization did not fully take hold. Indeed, there remained a strong market legacy, which enhanced the effectiveness of subsequent market-based reforms.
- The decision to introduce reforms resulted from an early recognition by the leadership that central planning was proving unsuccessful. This recognition was reinforced by the demonstration effect of the rapidly growing, market-oriented economies of East Asia.

- The Lao P.D.R. had normal financial and commercial relations with the international community from the outset of the reform process; in particular, multilateral organizations provided substantial technical assistance to facilitate the reform process.

Factors That Complicated Reform

The following factors unfavorably influenced the reform process.

- The institutional and administrative structure for implementing reforms was extremely weak and characterized by a lack of skilled workers, owing to the heavy loss of life in wars from the mid-1950s to the mid-1970s and to the exodus of educated persons and entrepreneurs with the advent of socialism. This weak structure limited the absorptive capacity of the economy, as was evidenced in the delays in both the effective execution of aid-financed projects and the utilization of technical assistance.
- The lack of modern tools of indirect macroeconomic management in the late 1980s led to temporary financial policy slippages soon after the reforms were introduced.
- The extremely limited statistical data base severely constrained the authorities' ability to monitor and analyze economic developments, and thus formulate policies.
- Certain reforms, such as privatization and civil service reform, were delayed because of their political and social sensitivity. Budget constraints limiting the scope for provision of a social safety net exacerbated the situation.

Future Challenges

Despite the progress made in the past several years, the Lao P.D.R. still faces serious challenges in conducting macroeconomic management and making further structural reforms.

In particular, much still needs to be done in the area of structural reform. First, financial sector reform requires strengthened banking supervision and prudential regulations, increased competition, and improved management of commercial banks. Second, fiscal reform calls for an improvement in the structure of expenditure, particularly the prioritization of a rolling medium-term public investment plan—for example, through a *core* program—and the synchronization of this program with the annual budget. Third, civil service reform entails the identification, retrenchment, relocation, and redeployment of redundant workers, as well as the introduction of

a civil service examination. Fourth, the legal framework has to be strengthened in many areas, particularly those related to business activities. Fifth, land reform requires the issuance of land-use rights. Sixth, the trade and tariff system needs to be further rationalized, and the administrative capacity to implement the system needs to be strengthened. All of these actions are essential to increase the economy's growth potential and to improve the standards of living for current and future generations in the Lao P.D.R.

Finally, it is necessary to recognize that further progress in structural reforms, particularly those identified above, requires macroeconomic stability. Moreover, such progress calls for the authorities' sustained determination, as well as for support from the international community.

Postscript

Following the Government's reasonable success in establishing financial stability during 1989–94, macroeconomic performance deteriorated in 1995. Monetary and fiscal policies loosened. In the monetary area, the authorities pursued lax credit policy to boost private sector activity, which contributed to increases in the growth of domestic credit and broad money to annual rates of 61 percent and 39 percent, respectively, in early 1995. In the fiscal area, budgetary operations became problematic during the first half of the fiscal year. There were some overruns in current expenditure—on wages, materials, and transfers—while the collection of timber royalties fell seriously behind schedule.

These lax financial policies, together with a liberalization of imports, increased demand pressures. Consumer prices rose by some 14 percent (adjusted for seasonal factors) during the first half of the year, partly reflecting a substantial increase in food prices. Meanwhile, strong import demand exerted increasing pressures on the exchange market.

Initially, the authorities responded to these exchange rate pressures by selling reserves, depreciating the official rate by a small amount, and applying administrative controls, including limitations on the allocation of foreign exchange by commercial banks and on the activities of the exchange bureaus. These controls gave rise to exchange restrictions but did not solve the fundamental problems.

In mid-1995, the authorities decided to adopt a comprehensive policy package to put the economic program back on track for the remainder of the year. The central bank started to tighten monetary policy through direct and indirect instruments. As a result, monetary growth started to slow down; it is estimated to have declined to about 24 percent by the end of December. Likewise, domestic credit expansion fell significantly to an estimated rate of 25 percent by the end of 1995. Mainly as a result of monetary tightening, interest rates on auctioned treasury bills and loans rose over the same period to the 28–30 percent range and turned positive in real terms.

In the fiscal area, a set of measures—yielding a budget deficit reduction equivalent to about ¾ of 1 percent of GDP—was also adopted in June 1995 to correct the deteriorating fiscal position. Revenue measures included a strengthening of collection procedures for timber royalties aimed at recovering payments arrears from the first half of the fiscal year and securing timely collection in the second half, as well as actions in other tax categories. On the expenditure side, despite higher inflation, the Government cut selected current outlays (mainly for materials and transfers), as well as low-priority capital expenditures. As a result, the current surplus target (½ of 1 percent of GDP) for 1994/95 was achieved, and the overall deficit (after grants) was about 4½ percent of GDP, below the target.

In the external sector, the central bank adopted a floating exchange rate system in September 1995 after a period of exchange restrictions and successive devaluations. Since then, the market-based exchange rate has been stable.

The tightening of financial policies and the adoption of a floating exchange rate system in the second half of 1995 contributed to a reduction in aggregate demand pressures. Consumer price increases slowed markedly to an annualized rate of about 10 percent during the fourth quarter of the year; for the year as a whole, however, inflation increased to about 19 percent from about 7 percent in 1994. Output growth maintained its recent trend and was estimated at about 7 percent in 1995, primarily supported by buoyant private sector activity. The current account deficit (excluding grants) in relation to GDP narrowed marginally to about 12 percent, but the overall surplus was substantially smaller than targeted for 1995. Gross official reserves rose somewhat to the equivalent of about two months of imports at the end of 1995.

Progress in structural reforms slowed in early 1995, but the reform process accelerated later in the year. Following the establishment of a civil service monitoring unit in mid-1995, the authorities began to develop a computerized system for monitoring the retrenchment program, with assistance from the World Bank. Progress in other areas of structural reform included the extension of treasury bill auctions to the nonbank public; the removal of interest rate ceilings on loans (except those on certain loans to the agricultural sector); the further rationalization of the tariff system; the adoption of a new rolling medium-term public investment program; the announcement of a list of strategic enterprises to be retained in the public sector; and some improvement in the compilation of the economic database.

The policy slippages and the resultant deterioration in macroeconomic performance in 1995 clearly magnify the challenges that the Lao authorities will be facing in future economic management. This most recent experience seems to demonstrate that a prudent financial policy stance needs to be maintained while pursuing growth objectives and deepening structural reform. In the context of monitoring and analyzing economic developments and formulating an appropriate policy agenda, the Government also faces the challenge of making speedy progress in compiling economic statistics and improving their quality.

Appendix I   Real Exchange Rate Movements and External Competitiveness

Movements in the real exchange rate are summarized in Charts 6 and 7, which show the path of the real effective exchange rate (that is, the trade-weighted exchange rate adjusted for relative consumer price inflation) for the July 1980–December 1994 period.[41]

The Real Effective Exchange Rate and Internal Terms of Trade

The real effective exchange rate for state trade transactions appreciated tremendously in real terms between 1981 and 1987, as the fixed nominal rate (which was changed only three times between 1980 and 1987) was not adjusted in line with underlying inflation; this would help explain the weak export performance of many goods during this period, particularly between 1985 and 1987. However, the real effective exchange rate for various nonstate transactions[42] depreciated gradually on a trend basis, despite short periods of strong appreciation during inflationary episodes, as nominal rates were adjusted

with greater frequency. The real effective exchange rate in the parallel exchange market depreciated through the end of 1984 and then began to appreciate. From the unification of exchange rates in the beginning of 1988 through the end of 1994, the kip depreciated by about 90 percent in nominal terms against the U.S. dollar. The growth of consumer prices over the same period, however, was much higher, and the real effective exchange rate appreciated by about 60 percent.

While an effective exchange rate deflated by a consumer price index (CPI) can indicate trends in relative costs of living, it is not an ideal measure of price competitiveness. A more relevant indicator may be the internal terms of trade, which directly measure the price of nontradable goods relative to tradable goods.[43] An increase in the internal terms of trade would create a greater incentive for factors of production to move into nontradable goods sectors rather than export- and import-substituting sectors; at the same time, it would induce a shift in consumption from nontradable goods toward imported and exportable goods. Thus, the internal terms of trade can be a useful indicator of the potential impact of relative price changes on the current account balance.

An internal terms of trade series for the Lao P.D.R. was estimated for 1988–94 by dividing the components of the CPI into nontraded and traded goods, as suggested by Wickham (1993);[44] the ratio

---

[41]The real effective exchange rate is constructed as a weighted average of the nominal exchange rate, adjusted for differentials in overall price levels. For the Lao P.D.R., trade weights are derived from 1993 exports to, and imports from, the country's eight largest trading partners (except Australia, owing to the lack of monthly consumer price index (CPI) data). Nonconvertible trade is excluded from the calculation; thus, the real effective exchange rate series does not account for movements in implicit exchange rates vis-à-vis the nonconvertible area.

Because it is the only index available on a frequent and regular basis, the Lao CPI is used to calculate price differentials. The use of the CPI may lead to distortions if it is not measured properly. In particular, the Lao P.D.R.'s statistical base is weak, and the CPI is limited geographically and in terms of products; moreover, the transition to a market economy entailed continuing large changes in consumer items and product quality that are not likely to have been captured properly by the available CPI, with a probable overstatement of implied inflation. In addition, even when prices are measured correctly, shifts in relative prices and output proportions consequent to liberalization create serious index number problems; distortions of over 10 percentage points for inflation measures are not unlikely. See Osband (1991).

[42]Defined as an average of the various rates applying to private current transactions.

---

[43]For the purpose of this analysis, nontradable goods are defined as the sum of the value-added products, in real GDP at factor costs, of "livestock and fishery," "construction," "transport, storage, and communication," "trade and banking," "ownership of dwelling," and "public services," while tradable goods are defined as the sum of "agricultural crops and forestry," "mining and quarrying," "manufacturing," "electricity, gas, and water," and services of "nonprofit institutions, hotels, and others." Although these definitions are not perfect, they should be good first approximations for the period under review.

[44]In practice, these two indices are derived by dividing the CPI basket into those goods that are traded and not traded at prevailing prices. However, whether a particular good or service is traded depends in large part on its price. Thus, goods must be classified as tradable or nontradable with reference to a specific set of prices.

Chart 6. Real Effective Exchange Rates
(December 1979 = 100)

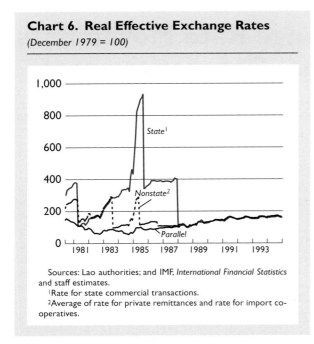

Sources: Lao authorities; and IMF, *International Financial Statistics* and staff estimates.

[1]Rate for state commercial transactions.

[2]Average of rate for private remittances and rate for import co-operatives.

Chart 7. Indicators of Real Exchange Rates
(1988 = 100)

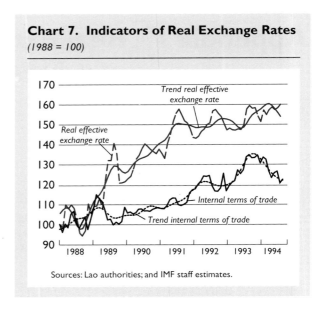

Sources: Lao authorities; and IMF staff estimates.

of the two resulting indices is shown in Chart 7 as the internal terms of trade. As measured by this index, the relative price of nontradables also increased between 1988 and 1994, but by 20 percent, as opposed to the 60 percent appreciation of the real effective exchange rate. The internal terms of trade and the real effective exchange rate have also differed with regard to the timing and magnitude of changes in their trends. For instance, during 1989–91, the former increased only moderately, while the latter appreciated strongly.[45] The internal terms of trade then began to appreciate strongly in 1992 and in the first half of 1993, while the real effective exchange rate remained broadly constant. During June–December 1993, however, both indices appreciated quite sharply before falling back in 1994.

Other Factors Affecting Competitiveness

Despite the overall appreciation in both indicators for the period shown (1988–94), which would have implied declining competitiveness in tradable goods sectors, output growth was strong and export performance quite robust; the share of tradables in total production rose, and the share of exports in world markets increased substantially. This development suggests that other factors, including rapid trade and payments liberalization and technological progress, overshadowed the effects of the real exchange rate appreciation during 1990–94.

First, the unification of the Lao P.D.R.'s exchange rates in 1988 at the level of the parallel rate probably produced an excessive devaluation of the kip relative to its long-run real equilibrium level because the parallel rate was very depreciated in relative purchasing power terms. Indeed, Chart 6 suggests that the "average" exchange rate (defined before 1988 as the average of the various existing rates) depreciated substantially in 1988 in comparison with previous years; this was particularly true for the large portion of trade transacted through state trading organizations.

The initial undervaluation of the currency implied a need for subsequent real appreciation to bring the real rate closer to long-run equilibrium levels. In goods markets, this appreciation coincided with high rates of investment and growth in tradables production, which set the stage for strong export growth in the next decade. Thus, if the initial incentive to produce tradables was very high, an increase in the internal terms of trade would not cause a loss in the competitiveness of tradables vis-à-vis nontradables; rather, it would reflect movement toward a more equilibrated level. Tradables production would still expand and remain profitable, despite the appreciation of the internal terms of trade.

---

[45]The slow growth in the internal terms of trade during 1989–91 is partly explained by the suppression of administered price increases, which affected nontradables. However, this does not explain why the internal terms of trade appreciated less over the longer period 1988–94 because administered prices later caught up with market prices.

Table 12. Tradables and Nontradables Production and Real Exchange Rates
(1988 = 100)

	1988	1989	1990	1991	1992	1993	Est. 1994
Tradables and nontradables production							
Tradables	100.00	119.23	132.02	133.47	145.30	153.39	168.28
(percentage change)	−5.22	19.23	10.73	1.10	8.86	5.57	9.71
Nontradables	100.00	110.90	115.82	122.09	128.80	136.73	146.42
(percentage change)	0.30	10.90	4.44	5.41	5.50	6.16	7.09
Ratio of nontradables to tradables	100.00	93.01	87.73	91.47	88.65	89.14	87.01
(percentage change)	5.83	−6.99	−5.67	4.26	−3.09	0.55	−2.39
Real exchange rates							
Internal terms of trade	100.00	104.99	105.96	110.44	119.32	127.31	123.38
(percentage change)		4.99	0.93	4.23	8.04	6.70	−3.09
Real effective exchange rate	100.00	118.09	129.54	142.51	145.38	147.19	155.4
(percentage change)		18.09	9.70	10.01	2.01	1.25	3.39

Sources: Lao authorities; and IMF staff estimates.

Dividing GDP at factor cost between tradables and nontradables gives an estimate of the supply response to movements in the internal terms of trade. The ratio of nontradable to tradable production fell almost continually, by 13 percent, between 1988 and 1994 despite the appreciation in the internal terms of trade (Table 12 and Chart 8). Considering that production in both tradables and nontradables also grew strongly in absolute terms, it is clear that the appreciation of the internal terms of trade neither hampered total output growth nor unduly directed resources toward nontradables. In fact, the current account balance in relation to GDP declined over the period 1988–94 (Table 13).

Second, the appreciation reflected the strong growth of domestic investment demand and the increased availability of foreign financing. The rapid decline of loans and aid from the nonconvertible area in the late 1980s gave rise to an increase in demand for investment financing from other sources; at the same time, an increased willingness to invest in the Lao economy is shown by the considerable growth of concessional loans, grant aid, and foreign direct investment flows from the convertible area during this period (Table 13).[46]

Indeed, strong efforts to increase domestic investment accompanied the large number of major structural reforms that were introduced in 1989–91. Gov-

ernment spending on infrastructure, although lower than in 1988–89, had a larger impact on the economy during 1990–94, as it was almost totally carried out with technical and financial assistance from the

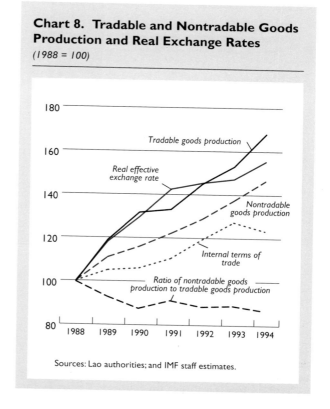

Chart 8. Tradable and Nontradable Goods Production and Real Exchange Rates
(1988 = 100)

Sources: Lao authorities; and IMF staff estimates.

---

[46]The increased availability of domestic financial instruments, together with declining levels of inflation and rising rates of return, probably induced portfolio adjustment and brought assets back into the country. This movement would also have contributed to real exchange rate appreciation.

Table 13. Balance of Payments[1]
(In millions of U.S. dollars, unless otherwise specified)

	1988	1989	1990	1991	1992	Est. 1993	Est. 1994
Exports (f.o.b.)	57.8	63.3	78.7	96.6	132.6	232.3	277.7
Convertible area	36.8	47.2	58.1	94.2	130.2	228.5	273.9
Nonconvertible area	21.0	16.1	20.6	2.4	2.4	3.8	3.8
Imports (c.i.f.)	162.4	210.7	201.6	215.0	265.6	410.7	528.0
Convertible area	90.4	135.7	130.7	210.4	265.6	410.7	528.0
Nonconvertible area	72.0	75.0	70.9	4.6	—	—	—
Trade balance	−104.6	−147.4	−122.9	−118.4	−132.9	−178.4	−250.3
Services (net)	0.4	4.5	10.8	−5.3	20.5	39.7	34.8
Private transfers	6.7	8.3	10.9	10.4	8.6	9.5	10.5
Current account (excluding official transfers)	−97.5	−134.6	−101.2	−113.2	−103.8	−129.2	−205.0
Official transfers	13.8	14.7	22.6	63.9	62.9	103.5	130.6
Capital account (net)	77.4	111.2	59.7	76.2	45.9	39.6	68.4
Medium- and long-term loans	22.3	48.5	45.1	36.6	63.1	48.7	78.4
Convertible area	16.3	38.3	43.7	38.9	65.9	52.5	82.2
Disbursements	23.7	47.1	49.8	47.1	71.1	57.8	87.8
Amortization	−7.4	−8.8	−6.1	−8.2	−5.2	−5.3	−5.7
Nonconvertible area	6.0	10.2	1.4	−2.3	−2.8	−3.8	−3.8
Disbursements	7.8	12.0	2.6	—	—	—	—
Amortization	−1.8	−1.8	−1.2	−2.3	−2.8	−3.8	−3.8
Bilateral trade agreements	51.4	50.4	37.6	2.5	—	—	—
Direct foreign investment	2.0	4.0	6.0	8.0	9.0	59.8	45.6
Deposit money banks	−27.2	−28.1	−3.6	34.9	−14.9	−35.8	13.3
Other capital inflows	—	—	—	10.0	14.3	9.0	—
Errors and omissions[2]	28.9	36.5	−25.4	−15.8	−25.8	−42.0	−68.9
Overall balance	−1.8	−4.4	−18.2	32.2	4.9	13.9	−6.1
Change in net reserves[3] (− increase)	1.8	4.4	18.2	−32.2	−4.9	−13.9	6.1
Net IMF credit (+ net purchase)	−3.4	7.5	—	11.8	8.2	8.3	8.0
Memorandum items:							
Gross official reserves[4]	0.7	1.7	2.3	28.9	41.1	63.3	65.2
(In months of imports)	0.1	0.1	0.1	1.6	1.9	1.8	1.5
Net official reserves[5]	−1.8	−6.2	−24.3	7.9	13.1	27.0	16.0
Current account/GDP							
(in percent, excluding official transfers)	−16.8	−18.5	−11.7	−11.0	−8.8	−9.4	−12.7
Debt-service ratio[6]	15.5	15.9	10.3	11.2	6.5	4.3	4.0
Medium- and long-term debt[7]	187.5	237.5	308.6	337.8	411.9	466.7	560.8
(In percent of GDP)	31.9	32.7	35.7	32.8	34.7	34.2	34.7

Sources: Lao authorities; and IMF staff estimates.

[1]Nonconvertible currency values are converted into dollars at an exchange rate of Rub 2.2 = US$1.

[2]Includes short-term private capital flows and unrecorded imports.

[3]Excludes valuation changes.

[4]Before 1991, official reserves were held for the Government by the state-owned commercial bank, Banque pour le Commerce Extérieur.

[5]Includes valuation changes.

[6]As a ratio of exports of goods and nonfactor services.

[7]Includes IMF; excludes debt to the nonconvertible area of Rub 796 million at end-1993.

convertible area. At the same time, increased confidence in the economy entailed large inflows of private transfers, particularly in the construction sector, as well as foreign direct investment. These factors exerted further pressure on the relative price of nontradables.

Finally, changes in the CPI were probably a poor predictor of actual changes in unit manufacturing costs in the Lao P.D.R. during 1988–94 because price and trade liberalization reduced the costs of imported inputs and eliminated monopoly rents, and widespread privatization enhanced productivity in the industrial sector. In addition, technological change may have favored the production of tradables rather than nontradables, as the former benefited from foreign direct investment, competition, and economies of scale.[47]

Moreover, civil service wages were constrained by the Government's wage restraint policy, while the strong privatization program and the restrictive credit policy held down wage pressures in the state enterprise sector. As in other transition economies, real wage changes are likely to have diverged from actual changes in living standards because the price adjustments were occurring in an environment of shortages.[48]

In the Lao P.D.R., the small depreciation of the parallel market exchange rate and the strong increase in foreign investment indicate clearly that recent changes in unit manufacturing costs were not as large as those indicated by the CPI. (Alternatively, those movements indicate that the level of manu-facturing costs in 1988, the base year, was artificially low.)[49]

Nonprice incentives may have also significantly favored producing tradables over nontradables during 1988–94. For example, foreign direct investment regulations were liberalized, quantitative trade restrictions were greatly eased, and access to foreign currency and banking services were substantially improved. These changes are likely to have significantly countered the possible adverse impact of the appreciation of the internal terms of trade on incentives to the traded goods sector.

That real exchange rate appreciation did not adversely affect the competitiveness of the traded goods sector is also supported by data on the market penetration of Lao exports. In volume terms, exports more than tripled between 1988 and 1993, when partner countries' demand for imports grew by only one half. Thus, Lao exports' market share more than doubled between 1988 and 1993, suggesting that the competitiveness of the Lao export sector did not deteriorate during this period.

---

[47]For a small developing country such as the Lao P.D.R., output growth is likely to be concentrated in tradable production, owing to the small size of the domestic market.

[48]See, for example, the discussion of real wages in Poland in Ebrill and others (1994).

[49]The Lao P.D.R.'s macroeconomic performance in the past few years has been very similar to the transition economies' of Central and Eastern Europe (in particular, the Baltic states, which have also achieved nominal exchange rate stability over a lengthy period). In the Baltic states, initial overdepreciation and rapid productivity growth led to high rates of real exchange rate appreciation without adversely affecting export competitiveness. See Saavalainen (1995).

Appendix II   Foreign Direct Investment

The reform strategy implemented in the Lao P.D.R. since 1985 has recognized the importance of external resources—both official and private—in accelerating economic transformation and in emulating the growth performance in the region. In particular, the improved climate for foreign investment that has prevailed since 1989 has brought several beneficial effects, including an increase in the level and efficiency of domestic investment through direct transfer of capital and technology, the development of new export industries, the dissemination of technological and managerial skills, and increased domestic competition. These favorable developments are expected to facilitate the further growth of the Lao economy in the coming years.

Changes in the Regulatory Framework

The opening of the Lao P.D.R. to foreign investment began in 1987–88, when barriers to external trade were significantly reduced, private enterprises were placed on an equal footing with state-owned enterprises, and a new Foreign Investment Code was promulgated, offering incentives and guarantees to potential investors. Three forms of foreign investment were authorized: business by contract, joint ventures, and wholly owned foreign enterprises. The Foreign Investment Code guaranteed that capital and other associated foreign-owned assets would not be nationalized or otherwise confiscated through administrative procedures, profits from foreign investment could be freely repatriated, and reinvested earnings would be exempt from taxes. In 1989, the Foreign Investment Management Committee was established to implement the Foreign Investment Code.

In May 1994, in an effort to create a legal framework for foreign investment at least as competitive as those in certain neighboring countries, the Law on the Promotion and Management of Foreign Investment in the Lao P.D.R. was promulgated as a replacement for the already liberal 1988 Foreign Investment Code. The new law streamlines foreign investment regulations and the tax structure and is consistent with other legislation passed after the adoption of the new Constitution in 1991.

Although the 1994 foreign investment law consolidates the principal elements of the 1988 Foreign Investment Code, it also includes several new elements that are expected to further stimulate foreign investment. According to the new law, foreign investment will be allowed in all areas not stipulated in a "negative list." This short negative list is likely to include such areas as national security, public health, the environment, and certain cultural activities. Moreover, the tax regime for foreign investment has been simplified, and a single 20 percent tax rate will be applied to profits (compared with the 15–50 percent tax rates provided in the 1988 code). As a result, profit taxes will be lower than those for domestically owned businesses, and, as in the past, reinvested earnings will not be subject to taxes.

For investments of particular importance to the country's socioeconomic development, the Lao Government may grant exemptions from profit taxes and import duties. Tax holidays for foreign investment can be granted for a period of up to seven years from the date of approval but are effectively limited to four years of tax-free operation after the start-up period. Import duties on production inputs and capital goods are reduced to 1 percent, and goods for re-export are exempt from duties. Import-substituting production can also be exonerated. However, companies involved in import activity will remain subject to normal customs duties. Finally, the visa procedures for foreign investors (and their families), including those on long-term visits, will be simplified, and all individuals associated with foreign investment will enjoy full freedom of travel within the Lao P.D.R.

Recent Developments and Prospects

Information on foreign direct investment in the Lao P.D.R. is based on statistics collected by the Foreign Investment Management Committee on approved foreign investment. By the end of 1993, the cumulative value of authorized investment projects with foreign participation reached $607 million, and about half of these projects were registered in 1992–93. By the end of September 1994, the total cumulative value of authorized foreign direct investment is estimated to have reached about $1 billion, indicating continued strong foreign interest, owing in part to the introduction of the more liberal law on foreign investment early in the year. Foreign capital accounts for about 80 percent of approved projects; in 1993, for example, of the total authorized amount of $159 million, some $133 million represented contributions from abroad.

Until 1993, the capital inflow associated with foreign direct investment was estimated to be quite small. However, these inflows increased from $9 million in 1992 to $60 million in 1993. The capital inflow estimate for 1993 takes into account the cumulative impact of past authorizations, the capital transfer associated with the registration of six new foreign banks ($17 million), the proceeds from the privatization of four state-owned enterprises ($13 million), and the likely underestimation of reinvested earnings. Most foreign investment (based on license approvals) is, in order of importance, from Thailand, Hong Kong, Taiwan Province of China, and Australia; it is concentrated in services (including tourism) and manufacturing, including the garments and wood-based industries.

The most promising prospects for foreign investment are in the mining and hydroelectricity sectors, which have the strongest export potential. A number of foreign companies and joint ventures have been granted licenses for mineral exploration. Petroleum and natural gas exploration involving U.S. and British companies has yielded promising results, and economic reserves of gas could be targeted for exploitation in some areas. Several Australian and U.S. companies have been given concessions to explore and exploit gold ore fields, and a company from New Zealand has already begun to exploit precious stones in the province. Concessions have also been granted for exploration and exploitation of coal and lignite deposits.

Four agreements for large-capacity projects to generate energy have been signed. Three hydroelectric power plants will be developed with the direct participation of the Lao Government. The Nam Theun 1 project will feature a plant with 210-megawatt capacity and is targeted for completion by 1998. The Nam Theun 2 project will require an investment of $1 billion and will have a capacity of 600 megawatts. The Houay Ho project (150 megawatts) will be developed by the Daewoo Corporation of Korea. Finally, a Thai company will be a major contributor to the development of the 600-megawatt Hongsa Lignite Power Project. All of these projects will be joint ventures with substantial foreign participation. After these and some other smaller projects are completed, it is estimated that, by the year 2000, the total installed capacity will have expanded by a factor of 14, while net electricity exports could be 17 times the 1994 level.

Appendix III   Legal and Constitutional Reform

Before the takeover in late 1975, the Kingdom of the Lao P.D.R. had the Constitution of 1947 and an essentially two-tier legal framework: civil affairs, such as family, dowry, inheritance, succession, land use, and related matters, were regulated by Lao tradition and customary law, while commercial business and administrative matters, legal procedures, and criminal justice were governed by laws closely following the French civil and criminal codes.[50]

With the proclamation of the Lao People's Democratic Republic on December 2, 1975 by the National Congress of People's Representatives, the monarchy was abolished. With it, the old legal system and the 1947 Constitution were also abolished. Given the resulting legal vacuum, the National Congress immediately elected a legislative body, the Supreme People's Council (later renamed the Supreme People's Assembly). However, over the next decade, the latter's role remained largely confined to ratifying decisions of the new Government, that is, the Lao People's Revolutionary Party. Lacking a new constitution, decrees and laws issued by the Prime Minister or a "Council of Government" started to fill the vacuum, but only a few such decrees and laws were issued through the mid-1980s. Moreover, decisions and resolutions taken within the party, albeit often not published, were considered binding for all citizens and thus became part of the legal system. Nevertheless, in many important areas, such as family or contract law, the legal framework remained largely undefined, and courts often had to follow prerevolutionary law. The situation was further complicated by the cessation of enforcement—without formal repeal—of previously introduced regulations and restrictions. Thus the emerging Lao legal system was difficult to interpret during 1975–85.

In the discussions on the Second Five-Year Plan preceding and during the Fourth Congress of the Lao People's Revolutionary Party in late 1986, the shortcomings of the legal system and the general lack of legal security were clearly recognized as major obstacles to market-oriented economic reforms and private sector activity, in particular, foreign investment. Consequently, the creation of an appropriate legal system was made a top priority. In February 1988, less than two years later, the Supreme People's Assembly (the first legislative body elected on a countrywide basis) passed an electoral law, and, in June of that year, three more major laws were issued that laid the foundation for a modern tax system, substantially liberalized the foreign exchange regime, and opened the country for foreign investment.

While plans for a new constitution dated back even further, to the Third Congress of the Lao People's Revolutionary Party in 1982, a constitutional commission to begin drafting was not formed until May 1984, under the guidance of a standing committee of the Supreme People's Council. In August 1991, a finalized draft was ratified by the Supreme People's Assembly.[51]

New Constitution

The Constitution[52] defines the Lao P.D.R. as a multiethnic (Article 1) people's democracy (Article 2), with a political system led by the Lao People's Revolutionary Party (Article 3).[53] In addition

---

[50]See Bogdan (1991); Norindr (1982); and World Bank (1994, pp. 98–101). Bogdan (1991, pp. 106–7) notes that in private civil suits the parties had the option to submit their case to a village chief or another local authority or to go to a state court.

[51]See Zasloff (1992, pp. 41–45). The Supreme People's Council, with 46 members appointed in December 1975 by the National Congress of People's Representatives, remained in office through May 1989. It was replaced at that time by the Supreme People's Assembly on the basis of national elections held in March 1989.

[52]The quotes in this section are taken from an undated Lao P.D.R. *News Bulletin.*

[53]In its Chapter I ("The Political Regime"), the Constitution is silent about the room for other, independent political parties. However, Article 31 in Chapter III ("The Fundamental Rights and Obligations of the Citizen") expressly grants the freedom of assembly and "to set up associations . . . which are not contrary to the law."

to the party, the Constitution acknowledges several other mass organizations, such as the Lao Front for National Construction and the Lao Federation of Trade Unions, whose role is to develop and protect the legitimate rights of their members (Article 7). Like all citizens, the party and all state and mass organizations must obey the Constitution and the laws (Article 10).

The Constitution guarantees a number of fundamental rights, including the right "to protect, preserve, and promote fine tribal customs and cultures" (Article 8), religious freedom (Articles 9 and 30), equality before the law (Article 22), equal and universal suffrage (Article 23), the right to education (Article 25), the right to work (Article 26), freedom of settlement and movement (Article 27), the right to bodily inviolability (Article 29), and freedom of speech, press, assembly, and association, insofar as it is not contrary to the law (Article 31).

The Constitution proclaims a multisectoral economy (Article 13), with all sectors encouraged to compete and cooperate with one another and all equal before the law (Article 14). Economic management is to be conducted "in line with the mechanism of market economy with adjustment by the state" (Article 16). The state protects "all forms of state, collective and individual ownership, as well as private ownership of domestic capitalists and foreigners" who invest in the country (Article 14), and this safeguard covers the right to govern, use, and transfer such property (Article 15). As to land, "which is property of the national community," the state ensures the right to use, transfer the right, and inherit it in accordance with the law (Article 15).

The Constitution establishes the National Assembly as the legislative and supreme organ of state power, with the right and duty to supervise the Administration and the judicial system (Articles 39 and 40) and to decide on fundamental national issues. The National Assembly is formed in general elections for a period of five years (Article 41) and convenes ordinarily twice a year (Article 43); between sessions, it is represented by a National Assembly Standing Committee elected from its members (Article 42). The National Assembly elects, with a two-thirds majority and for a five-year term, the President, who is head of state and commander-in-chief (Articles 54, 52, and 53(6)). The President's foremost rights and duties include promulgating the Constitution and the laws passed by the National Assembly; appointing or removing, subject to approval by the National Assembly or following a no-confidence vote (Article 61), the Prime Minister and the members of Government; and appointing, transferring or removing, on recommendation of the Prime Minister, gov-

ernors of provinces and mayors of municipalities (Article 53).

Although subject to scrutiny by the National Assembly, the Constitution assigns far-reaching powers to the Government and the Prime Minister as its head (Article 60). The Government is, as stipulated in Article 56, the state executive organ that implements the Constitution, the laws, and presidential decrees, submits draft laws, development plans, and the annual budget for approval by the National Assembly, and manages and supervises the Administration (Article 57). In addition, the Government is vested with substantial legislative powers, inasmuch as Article 57 (4) entitles it explicitly to "issue decrees and decisions on the management of socioeconomic, scientific and technical fields; national defence and security; and foreign affairs."

The judiciary consists of a three-level system of People's Courts (Article 65) and Public Prosecutor Institutes (Article 72), as well as military courts and prosecutors. The People's Supreme Court, the highest judicial organ, scrutinizes the decisions reached by lower courts at the provincial, municipal, and district levels, as well as by military courts (Article 66). Both the President of the People's Supreme Court and the Public Prosecutor-General are appointed or removed by the National Assembly on recommendation of its Standing Committee (Article 40 (7)), whereas the vice-presidents and the judges at all levels are directly appointed or removed by that committee (Article 67).

System in Transition

Rather than adopt another country's legal framework and make adjustments as necessary, the Lao authorities chose to create their own legal system. By necessity, this eclectic approach implied a prolonged period of transition, characterized by an incomplete and possibly nontransparent system of laws. However, lacking extensive experience with a market-oriented economy, the authorities considered experimenting and learning essential in the process of developing an appropriate legal system. This approach in part explained why, after promulgation of the new Constitution and elections of the National Assembly members,[54] certain urgent legal building blocks continued to be introduced in the form of executive decrees before a corresponding draft law was presented to the National Assembly.

Although a written constitution did not exist before August 1991, numerous laws were, in fact, enacted by the two predecessors of the National As-

---

[54]The elections took place on December 20, 1992.

sembly. The more important among these were the electoral laws of February 1986 and August 1991; the Foreign Investment Code of July 1988, which has been superseded by the more liberal Law on the Promotion and Management of Foreign Investment of March 1994; the tax law and the law on foreign exchange transactions of July 1988; the criminal code of November 1989; the banking law of June 1990, through which the Bank of the Lao P.D.R. was established as the central bank within a two-tier banking system; and the labor law of November 1990, which was revised in April 1994. Several other laws regulating, among other things, contracts, enterprise accounting, property ownership, and inheritance were also introduced in 1990. While most executive decrees issued during this period provided regulations to implement earlier enacted laws, two decrees issued in 1991 stood out as major steps in the reform process: the Ministry of Trade and Tourism's Regulation No. 112 of February 1991 on the Establishment and the Operations of Export-Import Enterprises, which effectively opened foreign trade to the private sector, and the prime ministerial Decree No. 91 of December 1991 on State-Owned Enterprises, which established the financial and managerial autonomy of state enterprises and the Government's rights as owner or major shareholder.

While in its first two sessions the new National Assembly concentrated on establishing its own procedures, culminating in the National Assembly Law of February 1993, important new legislation continued to be issued through executive de-crees.[55] These include the prime ministerial decree of February 1992 on the creation of a treasury; the December 1992 decree on land use and the November 1993 decree on forestry use, which extended important property rights while securing safeguards for the prudent utilization of the country's resources; the decree on land tax of March 1993; the decree on tariff reform of March 1993, which was a precursor to the customs code law of August 1994; the decree on enterprises issued in March 1993, which was eventually followed by the business law of August 1994; the decree on arbitration, the law on guarantees, and the enterprise bankruptcy law of November 1994; and the State Budget Law of August 1994.

Although the Lao P.D.R. has undoubtedly made substantial progress toward creating a legal environment conducive to its development goals, vital areas remain incomplete. Supported in part by technical assistance provided by the World Bank, work is currently under way on laws regulating secured transactions, procurement, mortgages, bank accounting and bank supervision, and negotiable instruments. While some of these laws are expected to come into effect during 1996, much remains to be done, in particular in developing the institutions and the regulatory capacity needed to translate the emerging legal framework into a well-functioning system.

---

[55]Since March 1993, the Ministry of Justice has published the texts of decrees, laws, and other important National Assembly decisions in Lao, French, and English in its monthly *Official Gazette (Journal Official)*.

Appendix IV Structure of the Tax System, End-1994

Tax	Exemptions and Deductions	Rate Structure
I. Taxes on Income and Profits		

Taxes on industrial and commercial profits (profit tax)

Annual levy on industrial and commercial profits derived by enterprises from domestic sales. Collected quarterly on profits forecast in Annual Plan; adjusted quarterly in light of actual outcome.

New and rehabilitated domestic firms are exempt from profit taxes for two–four years from the time that profits begin. Foreign and jointly owned firms are eligible for exemption for one–five years, as discussed below. Profit taxes on enterprises with turnover of less than KN 7.2 million per year are established on a case-by-case basis by the provincial authorities (*regime forfaitaire*).

All registered companies, including service, commercial, and industrial enterprises, are taxed at a rate of 45 percent. Commercial banks are taxed at a rate of 60 percent.

Minimum profit tax
(impôt minimum forfaitaire)

A 1.5 percent tax on turnover is applied in substitution of the profit tax wherever the tax revenue from declared profits is less than 1.5 percent of declared turnover.

Tax on personal incomes of employees

Levied on wages, salaries, bonuses, and other benefits derived from employment. Withheld at source by the employer on a monthly basis.

All persons with monthly wages or salaries below KN 15,000 are exempt.

Monthly Wage or Salary (In kip)	Tax Rate (In percent)
15,001–25,000	2
25,001–60,000	5
60,001–120,000	10
120,001–200,000	15
200,001–500,000	20
500,001–2,000,000	30
2,000,001–5,000,000	40
5,000,001 and above	45

Tax on personal incomes of persons in self-employment

Levied on self-declared monthly incomes of the self-employed.

None.

Annual Income of Self-Employed (In kip)	Tax Rate (In percent)
0–200,000	10
200,001–500,000	20
500,001–2,000,000	30
2,000,001–5,000,000	40
5,000,001 and above	50

Tax on dividends

Levied on incomes from dividends of shares.

None.

Taxed at 10 percent rate.

Tax on income from interest

Levied on income from interest other than from bank deposits.

None.

Taxed at 20 percent rate.

Tax System (continued)

Tax	Exemptions and Deductions	Rate Structure

Rental income tax

Assessed on all rental income; paid by the lessor when rent is paid.

Exemptions and Deductions: None.

Rate Structure: Taxed at 30 percent rate.

Agricultural income and profits taxes

Tax on agricultural income collected in kind for paddy and in cash for all other products. Following Decree No. 50 of March 13, 1993, this tax was replaced by the land tax, which is applied to land extensions (see below).

II. Taxes on Land and Real Estate

Death, gift, and transfer taxes

Applied to the market value of land and real estate property transferred through inheritance, sale, or gift.

Exemptions and Deductions: None.

Transfer Participants	Tax Rate (In percent)
Direct descendants	2
Second-degree relatives	4
Third-degree relatives	7
Nonrelated persons	10

Land tax

Yearly tax levied on size of land area. Tax is collected from January to end-April. Land to be taxed is divided in three categories: occupied land (i.e., land occupied by buildings and factories); agricultural land; and other.

Exemptions and Deductions:

Land occupied by temples, public welfare buildings, embassies, and housing for disabled persons (for extensions of less than 5,000 square meters) is exempt.

Agricultural land, not exceeding two hectares per family, occupied by disabled military personnel and civilians is exempt.

Agricultural land situated in mountainous areas yielding less than 150 kilograms of rice per person per year is exempt.

Agricultural land affected by natural disaster or other damages is exempt in accordance with the damage.

Newly cleared rice fields in mountainous (five years) and flat land (three years) are exempt.

Industrial orchards are exempt for two-three years.

Rate Structure:

For occupied land, rates vary from KN 0.5 to KN 10 per square meter per year in accordance with the use (housing, production factories, business or service, and unused open land) and location.

For agricultural land, rates vary from KN 500 to KN 6,000 per hectare per year in accordance with (i) land use (rice land, garden land, and farm land); (ii) location (level field and mountainous areas); and (iii) type of production (for rice, number of crops per year; for gardens, type of trees).

For other land, rates vary from KN 1,000 to KN 6,000 per hectare per year.

III. Taxes on Goods and Services

Turnover taxes

Levied on turnover of registered enterprises. Collected monthly on turnover forecast in the Annual Plan; revised quarterly in light of actual outcome.

Exemptions and Deductions: None.

Category	Tax Rate (In percent)
Food, clothes, medicine	5
Electricity and fuels	5
Consumer durables	5
Capital equipment, raw materials and spare parts	5
Jeeps and trucks	5
Precious metals	5
Construction	5
Transportation	5
Postal and telecommunication services	10
Alcoholic drinks and cigarettes	10
Perfumes and cosmetics	10
Jewelry	10
Consumer electronic goods	10
Hotels and tourism	10

Tax System *(continued)*

Tax	Exemptions and Deductions	Rate Structure

Excise duties

Levied on petroleum products and selected consumer goods.

None.
Specific excise duties

Category	Tax Rate (Kip per liter)
Super gasoline	53
Regular gasoline	36
Diesel and aviation fuel	18
Lubricants, grease, and brake fluids	18
Strong alcoholic drinks	400
Beer and wine	180
Soft drinks	50

	(In percent)
Ad valorem excise duties	
Cigarettes	20
Cosmetics	10

Business and professional licenses (registration tax)

Levied annually on registered enterprises, based on turnover. Payable during the first three months of the year on a current basis.

None.

Different rates apply to industrial, commercial, and import-export enterprises as follows:

Turnover (In millions of kip)	Industrial Rates (In kip)	Commercial Rates (In kip)
0–2	1,500	2,500
2–5	2,000	3,000
5–10	3,500	5,000
10–20	5,000	7,000
20–50	7,000	10,000
50–100	10,000	15,000
100 and above	15,000	20,000

Turnover (In millions of kip)	Import-Export (In kip)
10–50	10,000
50–100	20,000
100–150	30,000
150–200	40,000
200 and above	50,000

Land transportation fees

Levied annually on all motor vehicles (motorcycles, cars, trucks, etc.).

Government cars and cars of the diplomatic corps, international organizations, and foreign experts are exempt. A 50 percent reduction is given to government staff, soldiers, policemen, students for one vehicle, and a 60 percent reduction is given to pensioners.

Fees vary from KN 2,000 to KN 360,000 according to size of engine (for cars and motorcycles), weight (for trucks), and number of seats (for buses).

Air travel fees

Levied annually for (i) civil aviation registration and (ii) examination issuance and renewal of permits.

None.

Fees vary according to weight. Range is KN 7,000 to KN 70,000 for registration and KN 5,000 to KN 40,000 for examination issuance and permit renewal.

Airspace overflight fees

Levied on all aircraft, without regard to nationality, flying over the territory of the Lao P.D.R.

VIP special aircraft and hospital aircraft carrying patients are exempt.

Fees range from $160 to $250 per overflight.

Tax System *(concluded)*

Tax	Exemptions and Deductions	Rate Structure
River transport fees Levied annually.	None.	Fees vary from KN 200 to KN 20,000 according to size of boats.
Border entry and exit fees (for persons and vehicles)	Diplomatic personnel and relatives as well as foreign experts and relatives, are exempt.	For nationals, KN 500; for foreigners, $5; and for land and water vehicles, KN 1,500–KN 11,000.
Fees for extended residence in the Lao P.D.R.	Diplomatic corps, foreign experts, and their relatives, are exempt.	Fees vary according to length of stay from KN 6,000 to KN 12,000.
Fee for temporary border passes	None.	Fees range from KN 200 to KN 3,000.
Fees on delivery of passports, visas, and laissez-passer documents	None.	Fees vary according to nature of document and applicant. For foreigners, range is $10–$80; for Lao nationals, range is KN 300–KN 10,000.
Consular fees overseas	None.	Fees vary in accordance with the location of the consular office and type of document from $2 to $32.
Fees on possession of personal arms Levied every five years.	None.	Fees range fron KN 3,000 to KN 4,000.
Television and audio use fees Levied annually.	None.	For television sets, fee is KN 500; for videocassette recorders, fee is KN 1,000.
IV. Taxes on International Trade		
Import duties Imposed on the invoice value of the import following the GATT valuation method (yet to be fully implemented).	Goods imported as grants, inputs of foreign-financed investment projects, sample goods, and several other goods expressly mentioned in the implementation decree of the Customs Law (No. 1/PM of January 2, 1995) are entirely exempted. Goods imported by foreign joint ventures are subject to a duty of 1 percent.	Fees range from 5 percent to 40 percent in six bands (5,10,15,20,30, and 40). Higher rates are applied to three categories of goods: (i) cigarettes (60 percent); (ii) beer (80 percent); and (iii) vehicles (up to 150 percent).
Export duties Export duties were recently abolished with the exception of exports of electricity and some forestry products.		A 20 percent rate is applied to electricity export receipts.
V. Tax on Foreign Investments		
Foreign investment tax Imposed on declared profits of new joint ventures and private enterprises with foreign-invested capital.	Provisions are made for tax holidays. Foreign and jointly owned firms are exempt for one–five years.	A 20 percent flat rate is applied.

Source: Ministry of Finance.

Appendix V   The Lao Government's Policy Agenda, 1994/95–1999/2000

As described in the Committee for Planning and Cooperation's Medium-Term Policy Framework and Public Investment Program, the Lao Government's ambitious policy agenda for 1994/95–1999/2000[56] states the macroeconomic and sectoral objectives of the country as follows: (i) consolidate the macroeconomic reforms to ensure a smooth transition to a market-oriented economy; (ii) improve the efficiency and performance of the public sector; (iii) accelerate socioeconomic development and the improvement of living standards; and (iv) halt the degradation of the natural resource base. The policy framework's specific targets for the period are

- an 8 percent annual increase in economic growth;
- an inflation rate not exceeding 10 percent per year; and
- an increase in the ratio of public investment to GDP from 11 percent in 1993/94 to about 15 percent in 1999/2000.

The major challenges facing the Lao P.D.R. are in four key areas. First, macroeconomic stability needs to be restored and maintained by pursuing sound financial policies so as to increase both public and private savings. Second, structural and institutional reforms must be sustained, although the remaining reforms in this area will be more complex and more difficult in implementation than before. Third, given the strategic location of the Lao P.D.R. in Indochina, it is crucial for the Government to formulate its regional development strategy in order to benefit from the opening up of neighboring economies. Finally, a regional development program should be implemented in conjunction with social policies to improve living standards beyond the urban centers.

Macroeconomic Policies

Macroeconomic policies to be pursued in the coming years aim at increasing both public and private savings. To increase public saving, fiscal policy is targeting a continued increase in the budget current account surplus through enhanced revenue mobilization and control of nonessential current expenditures. Furthermore, to avoid recourse to bank financing, overall budget deficits are being financed by available concessional external assistance and moderate amounts of government securities sold to the public. To this end, fiscal management is also being improved along the lines of past reforms (see Section VI).

Additional revenue mobilization efforts focus on strengthening tax administration, mainly by completing the centralization of revenue collection procedures and improving the tax system. In particular, the Government is implementing (i) a comprehensive review of the tax system and measures to strengthen tax administration; (ii) an overhaul of the present system of royalties on the use of natural resources, including timber and precious and other metals; and (iii) appropriate remuneration of the Government's financial assets, including interest payments on its bank deposits and dividend payments by state enterprises on its equity holdings.

While containing current expenditure, the Government is pursuing a reorientation of expenditure priorities. To reduce the burden of worker compensation on the budget, further retrenchment of the nonmilitary civil service is being undertaken in the 1995–97 period in the context of a comprehensive administrative reform. A similar downsizing is planned for defense personnel and related expenditure. Meanwhile, an increasing share of current spending is devoted to operations and maintenance and social services, including health and education. The Government is also promoting a more efficient use of public resources by developing effective cost-recovery mechanisms for key public utilities.

To promote private savings, monetary policy continues to target positive real interest rates. An immediate goal of the Government is to liberalize interest rates completely, so that commercial banks can freely determine their own deposit and lending rates. While pursuing a tight credit policy, the central bank is continuing to enhance existing indirect monetary instruments, such as reserve requirements, the dis-

---

[56]On an October–September fiscal year basis.

count window, and treasury and central bank securities, to pave the way for the commencement of open market operations. Such a policy would contribute to enhancing financial intermediation.[57]

These financial policies should help mobilize the domestic resources needed to support increased investment and achieve a better macroeconomic balance. These resources, in turn, should help contain the inflation rate in single digits.

Structural and Institutional Reforms

The emphasis of structural reforms under the policy framework is on the effective implementation of the civil service reform, state enterprise privatization, further trade and financial liberalization, the strengthening of the legal and regulatory framework, and land reform.

Civil Service Reform

The main objective of the Government's civil service reform program remains to streamline the civil service while ensuring that compensation and incentives for the more qualified workers are competitive with the private sector. In order to implement the civil service reform effectively, the Government intends to develop a database and technical instruments to monitor the progress and costs of the retrenchment program and the wage bill. After establishing a computerized monitoring system, the Government will develop a long-term strategy for personnel retrenchment and relocation. In particular, areas of redundancy will be clearly identified, and a program to target reductions and retrain redundant staff and unqualified personnel will be articulated.

Privatization

Privatization will continue to be an important component of the reform strategy for state enterprises. Having identified several "strategic" enterprises to be kept under public control, the Government plans to accelerate the privatization process. During 1995–96, privatization strategy has shifted from leasing to the sale of company shares. At the same time, earlier leasing contracts are still being enforced, and parallel efforts are being made to reprivatize such enterprises—through outright sales or joint ventures—on the termination of contracts.

Trade Reform and Export Promotion

In the period ahead, the Government will largely complete the process of liberalizing the external sector. Actions will include the removal of the few remaining quantitative restrictions; the full implementation of the tariff reform adopted in early 1995, including improved customs valuation based on the World Trade Organization's methodology; and further rationalization of the tariff structure, with a view to lowering the rate of protection and stimulating export activities.

The medium-term strategy to promote nontraditional exports will involve the agro-industrial and livestock sectors and light manufacturing, especially the textile and garment industries. To this end, professional training centers will be established to help develop small and medium-sized enterprises.

Legal and Regulatory Framework

The priorities for the legal reform agenda will be to adopt decrees on procurement, negotiable instruments (bills of exchange and promissory notes), banking supervision, and other aspects of financial activity; accelerate the implementation of recently adopted decrees and laws, such as the business law, customs law, State Budget Law, bankruptcy law, and law on guarantees; and issue implementing regulations for several of the previously passed laws and decrees (such as the Foreign Investment Law and the decrees on land use and forestry).

Land Reform

The Government's recent initiatives to strengthen use rights on all types of land are expected to facilitate private sector activity. In particular, the decrees on land reform and use of forestry resources confer on all citizens the right to secure land use rights, while providing safeguards for the sustainable utilization of the country's land and forest resources. The Government is turning its attention to the effective implementation of the land decrees, and it has established several high-level working groups to address different aspects of the implementation process. Furthermore, a pilot project was initiated in mid-1994 to review property and title claims in eight villages in the Vientiane municipality. Drawing on the experience of the pilot project—which suggests, among other lessons, that the process could be somewhat more complicated and contentious in urban areas—the Government intends to extend implementation to all of Vientiane and subsequently to other regions of the country through cadastral surveying and mapping, as well as through the issuance of land use documents.

---

[57]An important step to enhance financial intermediation is to restructure the state-owned commercial banks after their recent recapitalization. The improvement of their management, as well as the revision of their accounting system, is a prerequisite for the development of an effective commercial banking network.

Institutional Strengthening

To deal effectively with the absorptive capacity problems that have hampered the mobilization and utilization of external aid, the Government is seeking to strengthen macroeconomic institutions and the database. To this end, as soon as the first phase of the United Nations Development Program project on expenditure management is completed, the Government will continue to strengthen the operations and training of staff in the government agencies dealing with economic and financial matters. In particular, it will ensure that budget and treasury operations are appropriately coordinated. Moreover, it will reinforce project monitoring and investment planning, with a view to maximizing the development impact of foreign aid. Finally, the Government will make strenuous efforts to improve the timeliness and accuracy of economic statistics to permit effective analysis of economic developments and to strengthen policy formulation.

Regional Development

The Government is seeking financial assistance from multilateral and bilateral donors for a number of important regional projects, such as road construction to encourage intraregional and interregional trade, an improved water supply for Vientiane and the provinces, and hydropower and forestry projects. The Government is undertaking a number of major projects in education, health, and environmental control in the provinces (see below). In this connection, the Government is also undertaking feasibility studies for projects to promote investment and trade links with neighboring countries, under a subregional development project initiated by the Asian Development Bank and covering Cambodia, China, the Lao P.D.R., Myanmar, Thailand, and Vietnam.

Social, Environmental, and Development Objectives

The Government believes that the key to improving the living standards of the poor is to provide additional income-earning opportunities and greater availability of goods and services through economic growth and increased production. In particular, the Government is stressing the provision of effective access to *social services*—particularly education, health care, and sanitation—which will allow the poor to participate in development. In the education sector, with the help of donors, the Government aims to improve primary and secondary education by improving teachers' salaries and student-teacher ratios, developing suitable curricula and textbooks, and improving the school network. In the health sector, proposed efforts include measures to expand basic health services, control the incidence of malaria, and provide essential drugs. The Government is increasing budgetary allocations for both social services and physical infrastructure in the public investment program. In addition, the household living standards survey, completed in 1994, and the forthcoming social indicators survey will be used to improve program targeting to reduce poverty and identify priority social programs for investment.

The Government's *environmental policy* focuses on zoning land and forest use to facilitate resource conservation; changing the incentive structure to favor resource conservation rather than short-term exploitation; introducing biodiversity preservation measures to promote production while conserving forest resources; and reducing slash-and-burn agriculture. With World Bank assistance, the Government has finalized its Environmental Action Plan, which will be the basis for attracting support from bilateral donors in this area.

The structural adjustment program (supported by the World Bank and the IMF) is likely to have a beneficial impact on the poor by facilitating broad-based *economic development*. It will be particularly important to integrate the half of the population engaged in subsistence agriculture into the market economy, so that these citizens, too, may reap the benefits of economic development. To this end, public spending on rural infrastructure will be increased, and access to, and targeting of, social services improved.

The Government also aims to minimize any short-term adverse effects resulting from the adjustment program. Thus, severance payments will help mitigate the decline in living standards from job losses related to the civil service retrenchment or the privatization exercise. However, as many civil servants are already augmenting their income through additional economic activities, the authorities do not anticipate a significant increase in open unemployment. While these factors may reduce the need for an extensive social safety net, the Government is actively assessing the need and scope for such a system.

Bibliography

Bank of the Lao P.D.R., *Economic Development in Lao P.D.R.: Horizon 2000*, ed. by Chi Do Pham (Vientiane: Bank of the Lao P.D.R., 1994).

Bogdan, Michael, "Legal Aspects of the Re-Introduction of a Market Economy in Laos," *Review of Socialist Law*, Vol. 17 (No. 2, 1991), pp. 101–23.

Bourdet, Yves, "Laos: Macroeconomic Stabilization with Trade Liberalization and Deregulation," Institute of Economic Research Discussion Paper No. 11/90 (Lund, Sweden: University of Lund, 1990).

Committee for Planning and Cooperation, "Outline of the Public Investment Program 1994–2000" (unpublished; Vientiane: Committee for Planning and Cooperation, 1994.)

Dommen, Arthur J., *Conflict in Laos: The Politics of Neutralization* (New York: Praeger Publishers, rev. ed., 1971).

Ebrill, Liam P., and others, *Poland: The Path to a Market Economy*, IMF Occasional Paper 113 (Washington: International Monetary Fund, October 1994).

Economist Intelligence Unit, *1993/94 Country Profile: Vietnam, Laos, Cambodia* (London: Economist Intelligence Unit, 1993).

"Laos," in *The Europa World Year Book 1994*, Vol. II (London: Europa Publications Limited, 1994.)

Norindr, Chou, "Political Institutions of the Lao People's Democratic Republic," in *Contemporary Laos: Studies in the Politics and Society of the Lao People's Democratic Republic*, ed. by Martin Stuart-Fox (St. Lucia, Australia and London: University of Queensland Press, 1982).

Osband, Kent, "Index Number Biases During Price Liberalization," IMF Working Paper 91/76 (Washington: International Monetary Fund, August 1991).

Pham, Chi Do, "An Unforgettable Experience in a Forgotten Land: Economic Reforms in Laos," Faculty of Commerce Working Papers in Economics No. WP 93/14 (Nepean, Australia: University of Western Sydney, December 1993).

Saavalainen, Tapio O., "Stabilization in the Baltic Countries: A Comparative Analysis," IMF Working Paper 95/44 (Washington: International Monetary Fund, April 1995).

Sasser, Stan, "A Reporter at Large: Forgotten Country," *The New Yorker*, August 20, 1990, pp. 39–68.

Whitaker, Donald P., and others, *Area Handbook for Laos* (Washington: U.S. Government Printing Office, 1972).

Wickham, Peter, "A Cautionary Note on the Use of Exchange Rate Indicators," IMF Paper on Policy Analysis and Assessment 93/5 (Washington: International Monetary Fund, March 1993).

World Bank, *Lao People's Democratic Republic: Country Economic Memorandum*, Report No. 12554–LA (Washington: World Bank, March 1994).

Zasloff, Joseph J., "Lao People's Democratic Republic," in *Constitutions of the Countries of the World: A Series of Updated Texts, Constitutional Chronologies, and Annotated Bibliographies*, ed. by Albert P. Blaustein and Gisbert H. Flanz (Dobbs Ferry, New York: Oceana Publications, 1992).

Recent Occasional Papers of the International Monetary Fund

137. The Lao People's Democratic Republic: Systemic Transformation and Adjustment, edited by Ichiro Otani and Chi Do Pham, with contributions from Jonathan G. Anderson, Michael Braulke, James A. Daniel, Filippo Di Mauro, Przemyslaw Gajdeczka, and Padma Gotur. 1996.

136. Jordan: Strategy for Adjustment and Growth, edited by Edouard Maciejewski and Ahsan Mansur, with contributions from Patricia Alonso-Gamo, Jean-Pierre Chauffour, Etienne de Callatay, and Christopher McDermott. 1996.

135. Vietnam: Transition to a Market Economy, by John R. Dodsworth, Erich Spitäller, Michael Braulke, Keon Hyok Lee, Kenneth Miranda, Christian Mulder, Hisanobu Shishido, and Krishna Srinivasan. 1996.

134. India: Economic Reform and Growth, by Ajai Chopra, Charles Collyns, Richard Hemming, and Karen Parker with Woosik Chu and Oliver Fratzscher. 1995.

133. Policy Experiences and Issues in the Baltics, Russia, and Other Countries of the Former Soviet Union, edited by Daniel A. Citrin and Ashok K. Lahiri. 1995.

132. Financial Fragilities in Latin America: The 1980s and 1990s, by Liliana Rojas-Suárez and Steven R. Weisbrod. 1995.

131. Capital Account Convertibility: Review of Experience and Implications for IMF Policies, by staff teams headed by Peter J. Quirk and Owen Evans. 1995.

130. Challenges to the Swedish Welfare State, by Desmond Lachman, Adam Bennett, John H. Green, Robert Hagemann, and Ramana Ramaswamy. 1995.

129. IMF Conditionality: Experience Under Stand-By and Extended Arrangements. Part II: Background Papers. Susan Schadler, Editor, with Adam Bennett, Maria Carkovic, Louis Dicks-Mireaux, Mauro Mecagni, James H.J. Morsink, and Miguel A. Savastano. 1995.

128. IMF Conditionality: Experience Under Stand-By and Extended Arrangements. Part I: Key Issues and Findings, by Susan Schadler, Adam Bennett, Maria Carkovic, Louis Dicks-Mireaux, Mauro Mecagni, James H.J. Morsink, and Miguel A. Savastano. 1995.

127. Road Maps of the Transition: The Baltics, the Czech Republic, Hungary, and Russia, by Biswajit Banerjee, Vincent Koen, Thomas Krueger, Mark S. Lutz, Michael Marrese, and Tapio O. Saavalainen. 1995.

126. The Adoption of Indirect Instruments of Monetary Policy, by a Staff Team headed by William E. Alexander, Tomás J.T. Baliño, and Charles Enoch and comprising Francesco Caramazza, George Iden, David Marston, Johannes Mueller, Ceyla Pazarbasioglu, Marc Quintyn, Matthew Saal, and Gabriel Sensenbrenner. 1995.

125. United Germany: The First Five Years—Performance and Policy Issues, by Robert Corker, Robert A. Feldman, Karl Habermeier, Hari Vittas, and Tessa van der Willigen. 1995.

124. Saving Behavior and the Asset Price "Bubble" in Japan: Analytical Studies, edited by Ulrich Baumgartner and Guy Meredith. 1995.

123. Comprehensive Tax Reform: The Colombian Experience, edited by Parthasarathi Shome. 1995.

122. Capital Flows in the APEC Region, edited by Mohsin S. Khan and Carmen M. Reinhart. 1995.

121. Uganda: Adjustment with Growth, 1987–94, by Robert L. Sharer, Hema R. De Zoysa, and Calvin A. McDonald. 1995.

120. Economic Dislocation and Recovery in Lebanon, by Sena Eken, Paul Cashin, S. Nuri Erbas, Jose Martelino, and Adnan Mazarei. 1995.

119. Singapore: A Case Study in Rapid Development, edited by Kenneth Bercuson with a staff team comprising Robert G. Carling, Aasim M. Husain, Thomas Rumbaugh, and Rachel van Elkan. 1995.

118. Sub-Saharan Africa: Growth, Savings, and Investment, by Michael T. Hadjimichael, Dhaneshwar Ghura, Martin Mühleisen, Roger Nord, and E. Murat Uçer. 1995.

117. Resilience and Growth Through Sustained Adjustment: The Moroccan Experience, by Saleh M. Nsouli, Sena Eken, Klaus Enders, Van-Can Thai, Jörg Decressin, and Filippo Cartiglia, with Janet Bungay. 1995.

116. Improving the International Monetary System: Constraints and Possibilities, by Michael Mussa, Morris Goldstein, Peter B. Clark, Donald J. Mathieson, and Tamim Bayoumi. 1994.

115. Exchange Rates and Economic Fundamentals: A Framework for Analysis, by Peter B. Clark, Leonardo Bartolini, Tamim Bayoumi, and Steven Symansky. 1994.

114. Economic Reform in China: A New Phase, by Wanda Tseng, Hoe Ee Khor, Kalpana Kochhar, Dubravko Mihaljek, and David Burton. 1994.

113. Poland: The Path to a Market Economy, by Liam P. Ebrill, Ajai Chopra, Charalambos Christofides, Paul Mylonas, Inci Otker, and Gerd Schwartz. 1994.

112. The Behavior of Non-Oil Commodity Prices, by Eduardo Borensztein, Mohsin S. Khan, Carmen M. Reinhart, and Peter Wickham. 1994.

111. The Russian Federation in Transition: External Developments, by Benedicte Vibe Christensen. 1994.

110. Limiting Central Bank Credit to the Government: Theory and Practice, by Carlo Cottarelli. 1993.

109. The Path to Convertibility and Growth: The Tunisian Experience, by Saleh M. Nsouli, Sena Eken, Paul Duran, Gerwin Bell, and Zühtü Yücelik. 1993.

108. Recent Experiences with Surges in Capital Inflows, by Susan Schadler, Maria Carkovic, Adam Bennett, and Robert Kahn. 1993.

107. China at the Threshold of a Market Economy, by Michael W. Bell, Hoe Ee Khor, and Kalpana Kochhar with Jun Ma, Simon N'guiamba, and Rajiv Lall. 1993.

106. Economic Adjustment in Low-Income Countries: Experience Under the Enhanced Structural Adjustment Facility, by Susan Schadler, Franek Rozwadowski, Siddharth Tiwari, and David O. Robinson. 1993.

105. The Structure and Operation of the World Gold Market, by Gary O'Callaghan. 1993.

104. Price Liberalization in Russia: Behavior of Prices, Household Incomes, and Consumption During the First Year, by Vincent Koen and Steven Phillips. 1993.

103. Liberalization of the Capital Account: Experiences and Issues, by Donald J. Mathieson and Liliana Rojas-Suárez. 1993.

102. Financial Sector Reforms and Exchange Arrangements in Eastern Europe. Part I: Financial Markets and Intermediation, by Guillermo A. Calvo and Manmohan S. Kumar. Part II: Exchange Arrangements of Previously Centrally Planned Economies, by Eduardo Borensztein and Paul R. Masson. 1993.

101. Spain: Converging with the European Community, by Michel Galy, Gonzalo Pastor, and Thierry Pujol. 1993.

100. The Gambia: Economic Adjustment in a Small Open Economy, by Michael T. Hadjimichael, Thomas Rumbaugh, and Eric Verreydt. 1992.

99. Mexico: The Strategy to Achieve Sustained Economic Growth, edited by Claudio Loser and Eliot Kalter. 1992.

98. Albania: From Isolation Toward Reform, by Mario I. Blejer, Mauro Mecagni, Ratna Sahay, Richard Hides, Barry Johnston, Piroska Nagy, and Roy Pepper. 1992.

97. Rules and Discretion in International Economic Policy, by Manuel Guitián. 1992.

96. Policy Issues in the Evolving International Monetary System, by Morris Goldstein, Peter Isard, Paul R. Masson, and Mark P. Taylor. 1992.

95. The Fiscal Dimensions of Adjustment in Low-Income Countries, by Karim Nashashibi, Sanjeev Gupta, Claire Liuksila, Henri Lorie, and Walter Mahler. 1992.

94. Tax Harmonization in the European Community: Policy Issues and Analysis, edited by George Kopits. 1992.

93. Regional Trade Arrangements, by Augusto de la Torre and Margaret R. Kelly. 1992.

Note: For information on the title and availability of Occasional Papers not listed, please consult the IMF Publications Catalog or contact IMF Publication Services.